Frances Trollope

Twayne's English Authors Series

Herbert Sussman, Editor

Northeastern University

TEAS 370

Frances Trollope

By Helen Heineman

Framingham State College

Twayne Publishers • Boston

Frances Trollope

Helen Heineman

Copyright © 1984 by G. K. Hall & Company
All Rights Reserved
Published by Twayne Publishers
A Division of G. K. Hall & Company
70 Lincoln Street
Boston, Massachusetts 02111

Book Production by Marne B. Sultz
Book Design by Barbara Anderson

Printed on permanent/durable acid-free paper
and bound in the United States of America.

Frontispiece portrait of Frances Trollope
by Auguste Hervieu from the fifth edition
of *Domestic Manners*. Photograph courtesy of
George Damon, Framingham State College
Media Center.

Library of Congress Cataloging in Publication Data.

Heineman, Helen, 1936–
   Frances Trollope.

   (Twayne's English authors series ; TEAS 370)
   Bibliography: p. 154
   Includes index.
   1. Trollope, Frances Milton, 1790–1863—Criticism and interpretation.
I. Title. II. Series.
PR5699.T3Z714   1984   823'.7   84–3771
ISBN 0–8057–6856–4

Contents

About the Author

Helen Heineman is Professor of English at Framingham State College (Mass.). She received her A.B. degree summa cum laude at Queens College of the City of New York, her M.A. degree at Columbia University on a Woodrow Wilson National Fellowship, and her Ph.D. at Cornell University (1967) on an Andrew Dickson White Fellowship and a Woodrow Wilson Graduate Fellowship. She completed the writing of her dissertation on an American Association of University Women National Fellowship. Between 1973 and 1975 she was a Fellow of the Radcliffe Institute, where she completed a biography of Frances Trollope (*Mrs. Trollope: The Triumphant Feminine in the 19th Century*, Ohio University Press, 1979). Her articles in Victorian literature, American studies, and women's studies have appeared in *The American Quarterly*, *The International Journal of Women's Studies*, *The Radcliffe Quarterly*, and *Harvard Magazine*. Her composite biography of a circle of nineteenth-century women (*Restless Angels: The Friendship of Six Victorian Women*, Ohio University Press) appeared in 1983. She also holds an appointment at the Radcliffe Seminars.

Preface

Frances Milton Trollope's life, alternating between family responsibilities and the demands of a rigorous writing career, moved steadily in a double rhythm of love and work. Even when she was a single woman with no professional ambitions, her husband-to-be noted what seemed to him unnecessarily compulsive behavior, such as reading Dante while hemming sheets. Much later when her children lay sick and dying, she was their bedside nurse and at the same time wrote novels to support the family. Eventually, when her life's greatest trials were past, she continued to mix domestic responsibilities, pleasures, visits, and travel, with the required regular intervals of composition. This doubleness became the pattern of her life, the wellspring of her being. Doing two things at once, she gave herself to each with greater intensity and clarity than had she had the luxury of undivided time.

This blend of activities helped her to avoid staleness and the writer's dreaded periods of silences. Once she began her literary life at the age of 53, her books came forth almost yearly, to the end of her writing career. Still, her biographers have often found her life so compelling, its struggles and victories so dramatic, that they have focused on her personal courage and allowed her literary works to recede into the background. But any complete telling of her story must follow the double rhythm of her life, and include accounts of her heroics as wife and mother, as well as assessments of her literary achievements. These latter had their own kind of daring and were often influential in shaping the literary landscape of the nineteenth century, in which she played a prominent and important part.

In previous accounts of Frances Trollope's life and works there has been a lack of objectivity about the woman and an absence of serious critical evaluation of her novels. Her daughter-in-law's adulatory biography *(Frances Trollope: Her Life and Literary Work from George III to Victoria)* and the autobiographies of her sons Thomas Adolphus and Anthony contain valuable family information, but fail to discuss her literary works.[1] Her subsequent biographers, whose volumes are described in the bibliography, have been careless about facts and underrated her achievements as a writer. Trollope has not been well served by her modern biographers. She has also been treated by the numerous biographers of Anthony, but most of them have either ignored her novels or treated them with mild condescension. The only serious critical evaluation of her work has been directed toward *Domestic Manners of the Americans,* but again, much of what has been written about her trip to America, the Bazaar, and her book about the Americans has been erroneous and distorted. This study aims at restoring Trollope to her proper place in the developing history of nineteenth-century literature.

Frances Trollope was an innovative author who explored a broad spectrum of evolving literary modes. While mastering the art of the best seller, she moved her readers to embrace an ever wider range of subjects and character types. Her books of travel are significant contributions to social history, eyewitness accounts by an astute observer who, utilizing fictional techniques, helped shape the genre. Many of her novels were path-breaking, and she set a tone of realism, satire, and social consciousness which other, often greater writers subsequently adopted. She was an early creator of a new heroine, strong and independent, preparing the way for more mature and balanced literary approaches to women. Her innovativeness is amply documented by the extent of critical wrath she aroused throughout her writing career. Concluding his section on Frances Trollope, Michael Sadleir asked, "Whence, then, Mrs. Trollope's power, fierce and undeniable, to infuriate contemporaries?"[2] While his study gave little attention to answering that question, this one will offer several explanations for that power.

The impetus for undertaking a study of Frances Trollope began with my discovery of thirty letters from her to Julia Garnett Pertz, a small portion of a huge correspondence preserved by Mrs. Pertz's great-granddaughter, Dr. Cecilia Payne-Gaposchkin. These letters were the first clue to how erroneous and even malicious had been many of the established characterizations of Frances Trollope's life. Since there were so many mistaken interpretations of events in her life, I was curious to know if similar problems existed in evaluating her works, often dismissed without serious critical attention. She had been depicted as everything from a frivolous bluestocking to a vulgar, manipulative hack writer. I decided to reconstruct her life, this time primarily from contemporary letters and accounts. I also read through all of her many volumes to find out just what that scribbling, sharp-eyed old woman had to say. In all my research into her life I acknowledge an enormous debt of gratitude to the late Dr. Payne-Gaposchkin, whose generosity in opening to me her family papers first inspired my work on Trollope, and to her daughter, Mrs. Katherine Haramundanis. In addition to those unpublished sources I succeeded in locating nearly 250 unpublished letters in libraries across this country and public and private archives in England. I wish to express gratitude to the owners and curators of all these collections for their generosity and kind assistance in my research.

The result of these investigations was my biography *Mrs. Trollope: The Triumphant Feminine in the 19th Century* (1979). The present work is devoted more to a scholarly analysis of her large corpus of works, all of which are, unfortunately, unavailable except in the hands of collectors and large research libraries. I hope this study will stimulate an interest in her writings, making reprints of her more important works possible. I am grateful to Professor Herbert Sussman, who edited this book, for his invitation to add this study of Frances Trollope to the Twayne English Authors Series. Though not the first in the long sisterhood of women writers, she was extraordinarily skillful at fashioning works which provided her family with financial stability, herself with a sense of worth and achievement, and her readers with books of respectable literary value. In describing her life and works I hope to make her domestic heroics believable, while leaving her considerable literary achievements undiminished.

Helen Heineman

Framingham State College

Chronology

1779   Birth of Frances Milton, second daughter of the Reverend William Milton, Heckfield.

1809   Marriage of Frances Milton and Thomas Anthony Trollope.

1810   Birth of Thomas Adolphus Trollope (died 1893).

1811   Birth of Henry Trollope (died 1834).

1812   Birth of Arthur William Trollope (died 1824).

1813   Birth of Emily Trollope (died at birth).

1815   Birth of Anthony Trollope (died 1882).

1816   Birth of Cecilia Trollope; afterwards Mrs. John Tilley (died 1849). Thomas and Frances buy Illots Farm, near Harrow.

1818   Birth of Emily Trollope, the second (died 1836). Thomas Anthony builds Julian Hill and the family moves to Harrow.

1820   Loss of the Meetkerke inheritance; rental of Julian Hill and move to renovated farmhouse, Julian Cottage ("Orley Farm").

1827   General agricultural depression; rental of Julian Cottage and move to Harrow Weald. Frances Trollope sails to America in November with Frances Wright, becomes a member (with Henry, Cecilia, and Emily, and Auguste Hervieu) of Nashoba, a slave emancipation colony in western Tennessee.

1828   Departure from the colony; arrival in Cincinnati; works at Western Museum. The Trollope Bazaar goes up in Cincinnati.

1828   Starts writing *Domestic Manners of the Americans*.

1831   Returns to England from America.

1832   *Domestic Manners*. The Trollopes return to Julian Cottage. First novel, *The Refugee in America*.

1833   First foreign tour, to Belgium and Western Germany. *The Abbess*.

1834   Bailiffs occupy Julian Cottage. The bankrupt Trollopes leave England and settle at Bruges. Anthony Trollope accepts junior clerkship in General Post Office, London. *Belgium and Western Germany*.

1834   Henry Trollope dies. Frances Trollope, acting as day and night nurse, writes *Tremordyn Cliff.*

1835   Frances Trollope in Paris, working on new travel book. October, death of Thomas Anthony Trollope. Frances returns to England and settles at Hadley. *Paris and the Parisians in 1835.*

1836   *Jonathan Jefferson Whitlaw,* first novel to attack American slavery. February, Emily dies at 18. Frances Trollope departs for Austria and Italy, projecting two books of travel.

1837   In Vienna; friendship with Metternichs. Early return to England because of Cecilia's illness. Works on *Vienna and the Austrians* and *A Romance of Vienna* simultaneously. September, anti-evangelical novel, *The Vicar of Wrexhill,* published. Decides she can earn more by writing novels than travel books. Begins *The Widow Barnaby,* female picaresque novel.

1838   Moves to London. Cecilia marries John Tilley.

1839   Travels to Manchester to collect materials for a book on "the condition of the factory hands," *Michael Armstrong, the Factory Boy,* published in monthly parts. Buys land in Penrith, plans house to live near Cecilia. Fifth edition of *Domestic Manners.* Paris expedition with Anthony.

1840   Birth of Cecilia's first child, Frances Trollope Tilley. Serial publication of *The Widow Married,* a sequel to *The Widow Barnaby. One Fault* published; also *The Ward of Thorpe Combe.* Anthony Trollope seriously ill, nursed by his mother in London. She completes two serialized novels of London Life, *Charles Chesterfield* and *The Blue Belles of England.*

1842   Makes long-projected trip to Italy. *A Visit to Italy.* Anthony becomes Deputy Postal Surveyor at Banagher in Ireland. Mrs. Trollope completes new house at Penrith, Carlton Hill.

1843   Brings back the Barnaby characters a third time in a fictionalization of her American experiences, *The Barnabys in America.* Gives up house to the Tilleys; she and Tom will live a year in Florence. Completes the parts of *Jessie Phillips,* her attack on the new Poor Law, especially the bastardy clauses. *The Laurringtons.*

1844   Anthony Trollope marries Rose Heseltine. Frances attends wedding; agrees to place Anthony's manuscript of an Irish novel with a publisher. September, returns to Florence. *Young Love.*

1846   *The Attractive Man, The Robertses on Their Travels, Travels and Travelers,* her 20th, 21st, and 22d novels. Begins a tour of the Tyrol, Bohemia, and Silesia with Tom and friends.

1847   Anti-Jesuit novel, *Father Eustace.* Anthony publishes *The Macdermots of Ballycloran* and is writing *The Kellys and the O'Kellys,* novels of Irish life. *The Three Cousins.* September, Cecilia is ordered to spend two years in Italy to recover her health. Mrs. Trollope nurses her.

1848   Tom marries Theodosia Garrow. Cecilia returns to England, her condition pronounced hopeless. *Town and Country. The Young Countess.*

1849   Cecilia dies April 10. *The Lottery of Marriage* and *The Old World and the New.* Visits Anthony in Ireland.

1850   *Petticoat Government.* Begins last period of her writing career.

1851   *Second Love* and *Mrs. Mathews.*

1852   *Uncle Walter,* 30th novel.

1853   Tom's child born, Beatrice (Bice) Trollope. *The Young Heiress.*

1854   *The Life and Adventures of a Clever Woman.*

1856   Last novel, *Fashionable Life: or Paris and London.* In bad health and attracted by mesmerism and seances.

1857   Anthony publishes *Barchester Towers.*

1863   Dies in Florence. Her last words: "Poor Cecilia!"

Chapter One
Frances Trollope: The Life
Youth and Marriage

In the years before her marriage at age thirty, little outwardly distinguished the life of Frances Milton from that of many other young women of her time. Perhaps its most dramatic features were the early death of her mother and the somewhat eccentric character of her clergyman father. Indeed, as if the combination were a kind of formula for success, some other women of her day who went on to literary careers—Clara Reeve, Anna Barbauld, Jane Austen, and the Brontë sisters—shared this background. All these women were the daughters of clergymen, who taught them and whose mothers died early or played merely peripheral roles in their education. This combination of circumstances seemed promising for the development of the nineteenth-century literary woman of independent mind and unconventional nature,[1] providing a solid, if somewhat unfocused education together with a lack of emphasis on marital prospects and domestic duties.

Clearly, the dominant figure in the early life of Frances Milton was her father, the Reverend William Milton, who became for her both model and mentor. He was a graduate of Winchester and Oxford, a man of good classical training and manifold scientific interests, whose most delightful hours were not spent writing sermons, but solving mathematical problems and designing an eclectic range of complicated gadgetry. Taken together, his inventions aimed at achieving a comfortable daily life, free from petty annoyances. Only a man who enjoyed the pleasures of the table would be prompted to design, as he did, a porcelain dinner service inset with silver pieces to deaden the sound of knives scratching dishes while cutting. To make traveling more amiable, he contrived devices to prevent stagecoaches from upsetting. For many years he worked at a plan to redesign the port of Bristol which, even though another was ultimately adopted, was nevertheless commended by the town fathers.

In all his three children, Mary, Frances, and Henry, the Reverend
Milton fostered a love of learning and culture. There was great
freedom of thought and ample educational opportunity for all of
them. Frances took advantage of her father's large library and read
widely in literature, art, and foreign languages, and mastered French,
Italian, and Latin under his sporadic tutelage. Most important, she
developed a facility for writing and a clear English prose style. From
all reports, her father was a cheerful man, whose interest in the
good things of this life, as well as of the next, endeared him to his
parish and family alike. Frances inherited his sunny, optimistic
temperament, her strongest defense against later adversities, as well
as his robust constitution and strong habits of independence. With
no mother to direct Frances and her sister Mary toward the usual
concentration on feminine interests and domestic activities, the par-
sonage at Heckfield became an intellectual hothouse for the clever,
lively Frances.

Until she was twenty-one, life proceeded in pleasant fashion, the
Milton girls presiding over their father's social life and finding ample
diversity and stimulating activity in the family's alternating resi-
dences in Bristol and Heckfield, and in frequent visits to Winchester
and Exeter. But in 1800 a new law was passed requiring clergymen
to live at least more than half the year at the place where they
derived the income of their living. No doubt this change sent the
Reverend Milton and his children to a permanent retreat at rural
Heckfield. Sometime after their establishment at the vicarage, their
father remarried, and in 1803 Henry went up to work in London
at the War Office. Probably the stifling prospect of permanent
residence, plus the changes attendant upon the presence of a step-
mother, prompted Frances and Mary to move with him to 27 Keppel
Street, in the Bloomsbury area of London, to keep house for their
brother.

There was in the move to London no ill will, but rather a desire
to seek broader horizons. Frances herself, always closer to her brother
than to her sister Mary, found exciting companionship in her lively,
cultured younger brother and his friends. In London the young
Miltons entertained a wide circle, visited museums, attended concerts, and in general enjoyed their new independence and increased
range of intellectual and cultural activities.

Neither Mary nor Frances seemed in any hurry to marry, but in
the summer of 1808, after about five years on their own, an im-

portant event occurred in their lives. Henry brought home to dinner a serious young barrister named Thomas Anthony Trollope. Almost at once, Frances found herself attracted. She was, after all, almost thirty, well beyond the age for marrying. When his proposal came quickly, she did not hesitate, and after a brief courtship, recorded in a series of letters revelatory of their different personalities, the sunny Frances and the somewhat dour Thomas Anthony were married on 23 May 1809.[2]

During the first seven years of marriage, the Trollopes lived at 16 Keppel Street, where, in the normal pattern of life for women of her time, Frances bore five children: Thomas Adolphus, Henry, Arthur William, Emily I (died at birth), and Anthony. After the family moved to a larger dwelling at Harrow, two more children were born: Cecilia Frances and a second Emily.

Both her surviving sons, Thomas Adolphus and Anthony, later left autobiographical memoirs, and in their accounts their mother occupies the dynamic center of family life. She was teacher to all the children in their younger years, endowing those who lived to adulthood with cultivated literary interests. Thomas Adolphus wrote histories and Italian romances. Cecilia composed a clerical novel, and Anthony became one of the great novelists of his age. Indeed, culture was perhaps the family's most important household deity. Though the Trollopes were not irreligious, it was more important that the Virgil lesson occur daily than that the catechism be recited. Tom recalls being taken to the theater to hear Mrs. Siddons as Lady Macbeth, and standing in line four hours with his mother, who had with characteristic foresight brought lunches to sustain them. She regularly visited museums with the children and wrote family theatricals and charades for the amusement of family and friends.

Besides the fostering of a cultural atmosphere, her most important role in the early years was as mediator between the children and their father, whose increasingly gloomy temperament often made family life difficult. In the accounts of both her sons Frances emerges as the bright, fun-loving personality toward whom all the children were drawn. As Tom testified, "All our happiest hours were spent with her," and Anthony called her "unselfish, affectionate, and most industrious," stressing her "great capacity for enjoyment." Still, eager to be fair, Tom concluded that both his parents were "most affectionately, and, indeed, supremely solicitous for the well-being and education of their children."[3] In these early years Frances freely poured forth her energies, never desirous of any goal beyond family happiness and prosperity. As with many nineteenth-century women, it would take disaster to propel her into the activity of a personal career.

In addition to an ever-increasing family, life at Keppel Street and at Harrow was rich in friendships. The Trollopes were part of a wide circle of interesting and well-educated people. The house was often filled with visitors—the Garnetts, Skerretts, Merivales and Milmans, George Hayter the painter, Mary Russell Mitford the author, the Italian emigré exile General Pepe, and later the Drurys of Harrow School. Most of these were Mrs. Trollope's friends, especially the women, with whom she maintained close relationships across a lifetime. From the Harrow days, when, according to Tom, she was always a special friend to all the young girls, to the end of her life and her friendships with the illustrious Madame Recamier, Mme de Chateaubriand, Princess Metternich, Rosina Bulwer, and others, she was close to clever and cultivated women. Cultural activities, family, friends, involvement in local controversies like her antagonism toward the Vicar, "Velvet Cunningham," and the debate over the burial of Byron's illegitimate daughter at Harrow, kept Frances happily occupied until the first financial troubles began to emerge, soon after the family's move to Harrow.

In 1818, Thomas Trollope made financial arrangements that were to have far-reaching consequences for the whole family. Feeling himself able to support a country house as well as his Keppel Street dwelling, he took a twenty-five-year lease on a farm in Harrow, owned by John, Lord Northwick, on fairly favorable rental terms. There Mr. Trollope built a splendid house, the cost of which was covered by a mortgage financed by a reduction in the farm's annual rents. This arrangement, often misunderstood and criticized as foolish by later biographers and by his own sons, was meant to be only temporary and mutually beneficial to Lord Northwick and Thomas Anthony, who planned to live in this house only until his elderly and childless uncle Adolphus Meetkerke died. Then, as the heir, he would move the family to the large estate in Hertfordshire. Young Thomas Adolphus, appropriately named after Meetkerke, had even been brought to meet the tenantry as the future owner. Unfortunately, these plans went awry when the newly widowed uncle unexpectedly remarried and almost at once began to produce heirs, crushing the Trollopes' hopes for the future. Under these altered conditions the family could no longer sustain their accustomed style of living, and letting their new large house to Mr. Cunningham the vicar, Mrs. Trollope's old adversary, the Trollopes moved into a rambling farmhouse on the same property, later immortalized by Anthony as Orley farm. Here they lived for ten years, trying to make ends meet with the combined incomes from Mr. Trollope's legal career and farming activities.

These years at Julian Hill were happy ones, despite first intermittent and then persistent financial difficulties. There was still time for parties, at which Frances enjoyed the intellectual atmosphere, sometimes wearing "her deepest blue stockings," and casting "Siddonian glances" on guests like the actors Kean and Macready.[4] Mary Russell Mitford remembered her friend during these years as "a lively, brilliant woman of the world, with a warm, blunt manner, and many accomplishments."[5] In 1823 the family went to Paris, in part to visit their old friends the Garnetts, then newly returned from America. There they were introduced to General Lafayette, who invited them to a ten-day visit at his elegant country estate, La Grange, where they met the radical reformer, Frances Wright, whose electric personality and utopian idealism were greatly to influence the future of all the Trollopes. At La Grange, Mrs. Trollope kept a detailed dairy, in which she recorded the highlights of her trip—museum visits, analyses of paintings and sculptures, rendered scenes of the elegant French country life. Her "genuine feeling for romance" and talent for sharp-eyed observation make the journal good reading.[6] It was an early piece of evidence—along with the Harrow charades, theatricals, and satirical verses on local subjects— that a creative power awaited some awakening. She had not written before her marriage, but the delights and trials of family life were beginning to stir her energies. This creative power, taken together with her natural curiosity and a need to record events, would soon generate a literary career.

Until 1827 the Trollope family fortunes continued to decline. With alarming regularity, Mr. Trollope argued testily with the clients he aimed to serve, making bitter enemies where he should have found helpful friends, and alienating even his children. His personality turned ever more morose, the cause of the change probably a brain tumor which produced dreadful, wracking headaches. His wife tried to continue making their home lively and cultured, but the situation worsened as a severe agricultural depression hit

all of England in 1827, completing the destruction of the Trollopes'
economic livelihood. Trollope could no longer pay his rents. He
resolved on more radical retrenchment and, subletting Julian Hill,
prepared to move his family into a ramshackle house at Harrow
Weald. With financial collapse not far off, Mrs. Trollope began to
consider alternate plans for survival.

In the fall of 1827 Frances Wright had returned from her utopian
colony in America to recuperate from a nearly fatal bout with malaria. She brought with her a deep commitment to Nashoba, an
educational experiment dedicated to proving the equality of blacks
and whites and thus eradicating slavery, "this horrible ulcer which
now covers a large half of this magnificent country."[7] All that was
wanting, she told European friends, were more recruits and a female
companion for herself. She had already invited Mary Shelley to join
the work at Nashoba, but the daughter of Mary Wollstonecraft and
William Godwin, and wife of the poet Shelley, tired of idealistic
schemes, had politely declined. To Frances Trollope, on the other
hand, the place seemed to offer an unexpected haven, where she
could temporarily escape domestic and financial problems and, at
the same time, find employment for her son Henry, unhappy at a
Paris countinghouse where his parents had thought he might be
trained in a career. Thomas Adolphus and Anthony were still at
Oxford and Harrow, but Frances, the girls, and no doubt Henry,
who was begging to return home, saw in Wright's project adventure,
occupation, and temporary respite from immediate problems. In
November 1827, to the surprise of all who knew her, Mrs. Trollope
sailed for America with Wright. Also among the family party was
the emigré French artist Hervieu, one of Mrs. Trollope's protégés
from the more prosperous Harrow days. He had been tutor in French
and drawing to her children, and she had admired his painting
greatly. Now he too was down on his luck and ready for new projects.
Ignoring the "dear me's" of friends and family, the large party,
with manservant, maid, furniture, luggage, two daughters and son,
set off on the rigorous 70-day voyage that would carry them to the
mouth of the Mississippi and life in the new world.

In America: "that land of plenty"

At Nashoba, Frances Trollope found problems more severe than
she had fled from in England. The climate seemed malarial, the

accommodations primitive, sleeping quarters in huts without ceilings on floors consisting of planks upon piles. Rain penetrated everything, and the chimney, made of logs and mud-plastered, caught fire with alarming regularity. The food was scant—no milk, no beverage but rainwater, a little wheat bread and rye, no meat but pork—and she worried about the health of her children. The slave population appeared demoralized and in no condition for education. The workers—Wright's sister Camilla and a few others— were in bad health themselves.[8] Most important, Nashoba's recently proclaimed philosophy of free love shocked this devoted family woman.

Thoroughly disillusioned, Mrs. Trollope left the colony within ten days. Without any funds for a return passage, she, the children, and Hervieu, headed north for healthier climes. Cincinnati, she had heard, was a flourishing Athens of the West and might be a possible residence until such time as she could return to England. Meanwhile, Hervieu began painting local portraits and Mrs. Trollope sought work, while awaiting a remittance from Mr. Trollope. He was himself now in desperate financial conditions, and ill and embittered by his wife's apparently erratic behavior, sent nothing and, for a while, answered no letters. Clearly, her fate and that of the children was in her own hands.

The only commodity she had to offer was her extensive cultural background. Predictably, she gravitated to Joseph Dorfeuille's Western Museum, which was just then trying to revive its own failing fortunes with extensions into new areas of exhibition. Mrs. Trollope approached Dorfeuille with two ideas which might loosely be characterized as projects in popular culture. The first was a spectacle called the Invisible Girl, an oracle which obligingly and impressively responded to questions from the audience in five languages. The voice of the oracle was Henry Trollope who thus found a use for his classical and linguistic skills which he had vainly offered as tutor or teacher. Mrs. Trollope's second idea was more elaborate, a representation in wax of scenes from Dante's *Inferno,* complete with demons, goblins, mechanical figures, and electrical shocks. In these projects she characteristically managed to employ all the talents of her entourage. Hervieu executed the artwork and figures (along with the Cincinnati sculptor Hiram Powers); Henry provided the sound effects, and Frances wrote the script and advertisements with

a dramatic flair that recalled the old days at Harrow. Cincinnati
residents were advised that

> Scenes of the Fiery Gulf and Frozen Hell, inspired by the illustrious Italian
> Poet, Dante, have been painted by the renowned artist, Hervieu, of Paris,
> France, under the direction of Mrs. Frances Trollope. Faithfully lifelike
> figures in wax have been executed by Hiram Powers of this City. Among
> these are Lucifer, Minos, Cereberus (3 heads) and Python (snake), all so
> faithfully executed as to inspire the beholder with the belief that they are
> living! The scenes of horror are awe- and virtue-inspiring! It may add
> interest to this exhibition to state that all the skeletons therein contained
> are those of Malefactors executed in Ohio within the past 20 years for
> their criminal offences.

Visitors were forewarned not to touch the wire surrounding the
exhibits "for the punishment for such temerity would be not only
instantaneous, but shocking!" One final "literary" touch completed
the program. In large letters at the bottom of the fliers stood Dante's
warning: "Abandon Hope all ye who Enter Here."[9] These modestly
successful attractions were still playing to full audiences long after
Mrs. Trollope had gone on to other, more enterprising ventures.

Encouraged by these successes, she now planned an even more
grandiose project, the Cincinnati Bazaar. This was entirely her own
conception, based on her astute observations of western American
society,[10] and funded with her own monies, an inheritance from her
father and her marriage settlement, delivered to America (by January
1829) in person by Mr. Trollope, with whom she had finally established communication. Mr. Trollope's cooperation in the financial aspects of this venture had been absolutely necessary, since in
nineteenth-century America married women could not make legal
transactions like buying land or taking out mortgages without their
husbands' approval.

The Bazaar was to be a commercial-artistic environment, a building housing rented apartments, businesses and shops selling all sorts
of unusual articles alongside space reserved for cultural events like
concerts, museum exhibits, and lectures. There were also to be
elegant entertainments—restaurants, coffeehouses, even a gas-lit
ballroom for dancing. Thus, at the Bazaar, general business transactions could go on alongside auctions of French china and alabaster
vases of the Medicis, club meetings of the Benevolent Society of
Cincinnati or the Lafayette Lodge, and theatrical displays by the

city's leading actors, the Drakes. It was an original idea, Mrs. Trollope's attempt to combine the American desire for genteel culture with their more natural commercial instincts. It was to be a temple, dedicated to the good life—both cultural and commercial. The building itself somewhat resembled a temple, in the Egyptian-Moorish style—and was the most unusual structure ever to appear on Cincinnati's monotonous nineteenth-century skyline, made of square, wooden-roofed houses, varied only by brick boxes with neoclassical trim. She commissioned Seneca Palmer to design the Bazaar, and its Egyptian columns, arabesque windows, and Moorish dome surely make it part of what has been called the "commercial picturesque" style of architecture. The building had three stories— a basement housing a barroom, coffeehouse, and apartments for commercial businesses; a main floor with a large splendid room for the bazaar itself, opening on a salon and balcony; and an upper floor with a ballroom whose arched windows and painted mosaics were in the style of the Alhambra. Surmounting the whole was a rotunda for viewing the city and 1500 feet of panoramic canvas decorated by Hervieu with endless vistas and portraits of local notables. It was America's most unusual specimen of architectural eclecticism and part of a national "Egyptian revival" as well. Later called "Trollope's Folly" by her detractors, it was an ambitious and even graceful design, whose potential can be inferred from today's dramatic use of recycled wharfs, warehouses, and breweries.[11] Combining the concept of twentieth-century shopping malls and museum shops, it should have been a success.

Unfortunately, Mrs. Trollope tried to accomplish too much with her bazaar. She had seen Cincinanti as a challenge, even as Frances Wright had regarded America. Nashoba might have succeeded as a slave emancipation colony. Instead, because Wright added to its original purpose a philosophy of free love, her conception failed. Mrs. Trollope's notion of combining cultural and commercial activity within a single building was promising. With an additional, albeit implied purpose of subverting the separation of the sexes in American social life, her project, too, collapsed.

In personal and business affairs Frances Trollope found the rigid proprieties of life in America for women very trying. Here, women did not usually enter the business world. Even in social activities like balls and dinners, women remained in separate groupings, eating with and talking primarily to other women. In her domestic habits Mrs. Trollope had often seemed bold and unfeminine to her Cincinnati neighbors—walking alone, engaging in business, living alone although married. At first, they had been amused, but then had snubbed her. Latterly, she had been called amazonian, a "man-woman," and the connotations of her name were used against her. Americans saw her bazaar as a dangerous and subversive attempt to change the entrenched patterns of American life. Activities scheduled for the bazaar were designed to mingle men and women in social and economic life. Even advertisements for auctions, for example, seemed directed at bringing women out into the public sphere. "In this country," the brochure stated, "it is unusual for the ladies to attend public sales," but because the articles at the Bazaar "are particularly adapted to the refined taste of the ladies, [their] attendance . . . is respectfully solicited."[12] It was this dangerous proselytizing attitude regarding the social habits of American womanhood that was most provocative to the Cincinnati audience she hoped to attract.[13]

But the Bazaar's immediate failure stemmed from an unfortunate confluence of circumstances in which Frances Trollope's radical behavior and "scandalous" associations with Hervieu were only a part. Equally responsible was her serious illness (an attack of malaria) in the final days before the opening, when her guiding presence was most needed. An even more important factor was Mr. Trollope's default on a promise to send more money from England upon his return. This money, also part of Mrs. Trollope's inheritance from her father, he used instead to buy goods, "trumpery" by Mrs. Trollope's own testimony, and the unsellable merchandise, upon its arrival in Cincinnati, was auctioned off at once to pay the workmen's wages. The building was seized, and the mortgage foreclosed. All at once Mrs. Trollope's ambitious managerial venture was over. With it, she had exhausted her material assets, both in England and in America. The pattern she was next to follow was one common to the development of the literary woman in the nineteenth century. Facing the void, both material and emotional, she found the last resort was writing. One hope remained—the literary marketplace. To the writing of a travelogue-memoir of her experiences in the United States she now turned her last desperate efforts.

By the winter of 1830 Frances Trollope had entered into the darkest period of her trials in America. She told Tom of her frustration. "Everything . . . went wrong, spite of exertions—nay hard labour. . . ." Her lodgings and all her furniture had been seized to pay outstanding debts. She and the girls slept in one small bed at a neighbor's, and Henry and Hervieu lay on the kitchen floor. These privileges she obtained "for the value of my parlour carpet." Soon, alarmed by Henry's frail health, she borrowed money from Hervieu to send her son home to England. Hervieu paid all the bills in these trying days. What few possessions remained she sold to buy her girls shoes. Without either a room of her own, or a little money, desperation drove her on. "I sit still and write, write, write,—so old shoes last me a long time." Her only hope lay in her ability to transform her notes and recollections of life in America into a publishable product. More travel was also necessary, which would be funded by Hervieu's talents as itinerant portrait painter. And she did allow herself to hope: "It is *possible* my book may succeed."[14] By the summer of 1831 Hervieu's savings, plus a remittance from the Trollope family, enabled the party to return to England. Mrs. Trollope was returning home penniless, her only possession from the years in America the manuscript of a book— *Domestic Manners of the Americans.* Within the year it appeared to rave reviews and became a best seller. Afterwards, she felt for it the fondness Dickens later expressed for *Pickwick Papers,* his first success, and for the same reason. *Domestic Manners,* too, had quite literally made its own way in the literary marketplace.

Back in England

Her literary earnings from *Domestic Manners* made family life once again possible and even pleasant. On the strength of her royalties, the Trollopes left the straitened conditions at Harrow Weald and, no doubt somewhat triumphantly, reentered their farmhouse at Harrow. Not the mansion house, to be sure, but the comfortable rambling building Mrs. Trollope always had considered her home. Tom compared the changes his mother's return had made to those wrought in a pantomime by the sudden appearance of the good fairy. In part, her return had simply "brightened up" life. Materially, there was once again what Anthony recalled as "moderate comforts."[15] This renewed life at Harrow continued for nearly two years, while new editions of *Domestic Manners* and earnings from other writings permitted her to embellish their domestic existence with comforts they had all long done without: candles, pillows for their heads, and good tea. In these large and small ways it was clear to see: her long career as family provider had begun.

She knew, of course, that her writing must now continue regularly. In these years she formed habits of work which lasted a lifetime. Arising each day punctually at four, she wrote her quota of lines before most of the world began its work. *Domestic Manners* (1832) ushered in a writing career of twenty-five years, a new life begun at the age of 53. Her attitude toward her work had been firmly established in America. For Frances Trollope, writing was not self-expression, but salvation for her family. That initial focus gave her the necessary courage to persevere. Because further travel was too expensive, she began to mine her American experiences for further "good Yankee stories." Then, after the successful publication of her first novel, *The Refugee in America* (1832), she contemplated setting out on her travels once again, this time to Germany, where she hoped to combine business and pleasure, making another travel book and at the same time visiting her old friend, Julia Garnett Pertz, who had remained a faithful correspondent throughout the years in America. Thus, combining her writing project with an opportunity for her daughters to see Germany and gain instruction in that foreign language, the double rhythm of her life went on.

Her correspondence with the Garnett sisters was an important link in an epistolary circle of women friends with whom she remained in touch all her life. From America she had written Julia and Harriet accounts of her experiences and troubles. During her lifetime she would make several trips to see them, and these renewals (and countless others, mainly epistolary) sustained and inspired all these women as they groped toward significant occupation in a world in which woman's "natural destiny" was customarily defined as marriage, even while all of them suspected or knew differently.[16]

Even in the midst of her own publishing ventures she did not forget the needs of her friends, and tried to persuade her publisher and other literary associates to read Harriet Garnett's first attempt at a novel, also on an American theme, miscegenation. She grew more experienced herself, learning to shrug off criticism about her book, taking such remarks as her new friend Basil Hall (himself an author of a travel book on America) suggested, as "compliments to your talents and testimonies to your truth."[17]

After succeeding in making the trip to Belgium and Germany, Frances Trollope immediately planned a trip to Paris "to witness

the erection of Napoleon's statue at the top of the Place Vendome."
She had told John Murray, publisher of her German travel volumes,
of these plans for a Paris trip aimed to produce "such a sketch of
my tour as might be calculated . . . to excite some attention."[18]
Writing books that would sell was her chosen field from then on.
Besides the proven travelogues, she also produced several novels in
the area of social satire (a natural extension of her travel writing),
and wrote in the established modes of the Gothic and the Romance.
These apprenticeship works reflect her talent for social observation,
sense of humor, and a knack for storytelling, but are not experimental nor innovative. To earn a living for her family was her main
concern. As she wrote Tom during the early days of her new career:
"I must endure the present as well as I can, work hard, and look
to better luck in future for the enjoyment of what I may gain by
my labour."[19]

Maintaining this spartan, strict writing regime enabled her to
survive the next great period of trial soon to fall upon her and all
the Trollopes. She had written on schedule despite financial distress
and uprootings. Now she would master the sterner and more difficult
art of punctual work in the midst of searing personal tragedy and
loss.

To Belgium and Beyond: The Great Catastrophe

Despite the success of her travel books and two novels (four works
in two years), money at Harrow was, in her own words, "oozing
fast."[20] The farm continued to show losses, reflecting the generally
depressed state of English agriculture. Mr. Trollope was growing
steadily more ill (scarcely a day passed without headache and physical
pain) and was unable to work. Earnings from his legal fees had
almost entirely ceased. There were always the usual expenses—
domestic and educational—and Lord Northwick's high rent had
still to be paid. For several years Trollope had petitioned Lord
Northwick for amelioration of his payments. Now, cholera and
influenza ravaged the district, and most of the family was affected.
Despite Mrs. Trollope's continued application of her pen, financial
affairs grew desperate at Harrow.

Then, in the spring of 1834, the long feared catastrophe struck.
Lord Northwick sent his bailiff to make an execution for bankruptcy
at the Trollopes'; all their goods were seized, the mortgage fore-

closed, and a warrant issued for Mr. Trollope's arrest. With little
advance warning, his wife set about saving what she could. First
she summoned Anthony, who drove his sick father to the Ostend
boat. Legally liable for all the debts, Mr. Trollope had to leave the
country at once. Henry, never strong in health, was hurriedly packed
off to stay with his aunt at Exeter. Then, Frances, Anthony, and
the girls salvaged what they could, hurrying the family's "pretty
pretties" across the back hedges to their loyal neighbor and friend
Colonel Grant, who stood ready to claim the property was his in
payment of past debts. Anthony recalls saving "some china, and a
little glass, a few books, and a very moderate supply of household
silver."[21] For the young people the flurry of clandestine activity
seemed almost exciting, as they cheated the family ogre Lord Northwick with the gleeful relish of those who have suffered injustice.
For Mrs. Trollope it was the fourth time she faced total loss. First
the great house at Harrow, then the brief venture at Nashoba, and
the Cincinnati Bazaar. Now she had lost her lovely farmhouse and
was again totally destitute. Before leaving herself, she had enough
presence of mind to deposit the manuscript of her latest novel with
her brother Henry, whose task it would be to proofread it and
deliver it to the publishers. With bravado, she explained that Mr.
Trollope had "decided upon taking his family abroad for some time,"
and leaving the girls and Anthony with the Grants, she sailed alone
to Belgium to join her husband and seek lodgings in Brussels, a
location she had already settled upon for its cheapness and convenient
proximity to London.[22]

Her energy and resourcefulness during these trying days was truly
amazing. She had said nothing of these dramatic events to Tom,
who was studying for exams at Oxford. When she was finally settled,
she wrote him, again putting on a brave front, describing the Harrow
experiences as if they had been, not a defeat, but the lifting of a
burden. "We are, in truth, arrived at the *corner* I have so often
talked about, and if we can but turn it, things must be better with
us than we have seen them for years."[23]

At the Chateau d'Hondt, in a damp, marshy area of Brussels,
Mrs. Trollope, in "harass and fatigue" prepared for the turning of
that corner by once more transforming unsuitable lodgings into a
family home. Using the little she had been able to store at the
Grants, she made a few pieces do the work of many, and soon had
an acceptable residence. She worked quickly, for she saw the frailty

of Emily and, even more, of Henry, now reunited with the family.
Before long, the lodgings became a hospice for the dying. Henry
was first. Though always physically large, he had weak lungs. Soon
the unmistabable signs of advanced consumption could no longer
be ignored. In the winter of 1834 Henry worsened and became, as
is usual in patients in the later stages of tuberculosis, difficult and
exacting. His cough grew unbearable, and pain and hunger constantly wracked his body. Irritable and impatient, he wanted his
mother during all his waking hours. Only when he slept fitfully
could she work, this time on another novel, a task she accomplished
by dosing herself with strong green tea to stay awake for writing
on alternate nights. As his condition worsened, she sent the others
away. Cecilia went to the Henry Miltons, and Anthony got a job
at the London Post Office through his mother's friend Mrs. Francis
Freeling. Tom was already at Birmingham in a teaching position.
Emily was too frail to be sent anywhere and Mr. Trollope was himself
an invalid. Finally, in December 1834 Henry died, and Mrs. Trollope called her family home.

A few months later she set out upon another writing trip, this
time to Paris, where she saw the Garnetts again and researched
another travel book. The journey was therapy after the terrible
winter, but her sufferings were not over. By October 1835 Mr.
Trollope himself was dead. His son Anthony later would meditate
upon the "adverse fate" of this fundamentally good man, "finely
educated, of great parts, with immense capacity for work, physically
strong . . . , addicted to no vices, carried off by no pleasures,
affectionate by nature . . . , born to fair fortunes," for whom
everything had gone wrong. His life, Anthony concluded, "was one
long tragedy."[24] For his widow there was not even time to grieve.
In February 1836, in another swift stroke, Emily died of the consumption that had killed Henry. In a little over a year, Frances
Trollope had nursed in mortal illness her twenty-year-old son, her
husband, and eighteen-year-old daughter. In that same period—
from Christmas 1834 to Spring 1836—she had completed *Tremordyn
Cliff* (1835), *Paris and the Parisians in 1835* (1836), and one of her
best novels, the antislavery book, *Jonathan Jefferson Whitlaw* (1836).
Her son Anthony, himself to follow a rigorously disciplined writing
schedule, later testified to his mother's truly amazing ability to keep
"her intellect by itself clear from the troubles of the world, and fit
for the duty it had to do." Her growing readership knew little of

her personal tragedies. Even her family came to take for granted
the steady stream of publication. "The novels went on, of course,"
Anthony recalled. "We had already learned to know that they would
be forthcoming at stated intervals,—and they always were forthcoming."[25] Her writing career, begun as a response to financial
disaster and an outlet for creative energy, now became the thera-
peutic discipline that brought her through personal disasters.

Safe Waters: Security

After these deaths, Frances Trollope established herself in England, safe now from all creditors. She had furnished a house at
Hadley in 1835, and after Emily's death she again established a
healthy rhythm of life for the survivors. Anthony recalled "how gay
she made the place with little dinners, little dances, and little
picnics, while she herself was at work every morning long before
others had left their beds."[26]

She made two more journeys in search of travel material. The
first was to Austria in 1837; from it she gleaned a travel book, a
novel, the friendship of the Metternichs, and in increasingly conservative political outlook. The Trollopes—Frances, Tom, and Cecilia—stayed six weeks in Vienna, where the frantic pace of balls,
dinners, and late-night entertainments began to tell upon Cecilia.
Frightened by signs of a decline in her daughter's health, Mrs.
Trollope returned to England instead of extending the trip to Italy,
as had originally been planned. In 1838 she moved to London, to
be nearer her literary work. Travel as a focal point of her life was
passing away. Ever since she had set sail for America in 1827, she
had been something of a wanderer. For fifteen years she had moved
from one residence to another. Indeed, Anthony calculated that she
had "established and re-established herself six times in 10 years."
Provoked sometimes by debt, sometimes by the needs of her children, often by her own searches for congenial company and locales,
she had gone from place to place.

Now all her children were settled. Anthony had come through a
period of nearly suicidal depression, had married, and started writing
his own novels—that great palliative of the Trollopes. Cecilia had
fallen in love with Anthony's friend John Tilley, had married, and
was living happily at Penrith. Indeed, Frances Trollope herself had
begun to build a house near Cecilia. Tom had resigned his Bir-

mingham appointment and joined his mother as her companion. They were happily planning the landscaping and furnishings of Carlton Hill when, all at once, the old restlessness returned. Thoughts of the cancelled Italian trip surfaced and finally, she and Tom decided upon a year's residence in Italy. After living barely six months at Carlton Hill, she began a unique journey, the only one of her trips unalloyed by personal unhappiness or pressing financial considerations. From it she made a travel book which, predictably, lacked the customary critical eye. More important, she found a permanent home in Italy, which had long been for her, as it had been for Byron, that "greenest isle of the imagination."

This relatively peaceful period, from 1837 to 1842, was one of great literary productivity. In these years not only did the quantity of her works earn her a place in the literary history of her era, but her willingness to explore subjects not previously treated in polite fiction was notable and courageous. Negro slavery, prurient evangelical fervor, child labor in the northern factories, and the "fallen woman" all found their way into her fiction. Indeed, in 1838, when she met Charles Dickens, there was an immediate and strong sympathy between these two reformers who had each in different ways sought to stir the public to indignation about some of the more unpleasant realities of nineteenth-century life.

The new freedom from pressing financial cares left her literary imagination more relaxed than it had been in years. In this period she became increasingly more inventive in the development of the female character in her novels. Her originality manifested itself in depictions of women as strong, aggressive, even "vulgar" characters who were harmonious with her deep awareness of her own female experience, at odds with the sweet, submissive types then current in popular literature. Here, she provoked critical attacks much in the same way as did the Brontë sisters. But personal tragedies had toughened her, and critical spleen meant little to the woman who had survived the loss of home, house, and family several times over. Besides, her obvious popularity with readers confirmed her own sense that, while her plots might sometimes creak, and the linguistic surfaces of her books lack the poetic suggestiveness of a Dickens, her characters at any rate had an authenticity and a freshness that were attractive and compelling. Once pleasantly ensconced in Florence with the beloved Tom, the companion of so many previous

travels, she continued to "rule the circulating libraries from the
Orkneys to Land's End."[27]

She also became a busy hostess in a city that was a must for
English travelers and expatriates. Robert and Elizabeth Browning,
having read some of the critical attacks on Mrs. Trollope, anticipated
the worst of her and were pleasantly surprised when they joined the
Anglo-Florentine culture in 1846. Later, her daughter-in-law wrote
of her popularity with all kinds of people: "She had admirably good
sense, much genuine humour, great knowledge of the world, and
a quick appreciation of others' gifts, and above all, a character of
the most flawless sincerity, and a warmly affectionate heart."[28]

Despite distance, she remained close to all her family. With the
Tilleys she alternated between family reunions at Carlton Hill in
Penrith (where Cecilia and family had removed) and a regular correspondence, complete with gifts of handmade dolls' dresses for her
granddaughter Frances Trollope Tilley and her sisters and brother.
The Anthony Trollopes frequently came to Italy for visits. In 1895
Tom's second wife wrote a biography of the mother-in-law she had
never known, basing it largely on the letters Frances Trollope had
exchanged with family and friends. Running alongside the depiction
of a successful and industrious novelist emerged another portrait
"essentially womanly." And, "although from circumstances, she was
in her day distinguished by a great deal of public notice, the really
happy moments of her life were those passed in her home, amid
home affections and home interests."[29] The double rhythm of love
and work continued to pulsate across her entire life, which now
seemed a matter of the regular production of the books she loved
to write and intercourse with the family members she had succeeded
in bringing through the arduous days of the past. But one more
trial awaited Frances Trollope.

One More Trial

Sometime in August 1847 she grew alarmed about Cecilia's health.
Since her marriage, Cecilia had borne five children in rapid succession, and her constitution, never as strong as her mother's, began
to show signs of the consumption that had already claimed two of
her brothers and a sister. To restore her health, doctors ordered her
to spend two years in a warm climate, then the typical remedy for
tuberculosis. When John Tilley wrote of Cecilia's condition, her

mother, with characteristic selflessness, arranged for Cecilia to stay with her. In September 1847 Cecilia arrived in Florence, where the winter climate was immediately declared too severe. At once, Mrs. Trollope took apartments in Rome and moved there with her daughter. But despite all efforts, Cecilia grew weaker, and soon could not walk even a short distance. By May 1848 the doctors declared the Italian climate ineffective. As she was longing sadly after her husband and children, it was decided that she return to her home, where she arrived considerably weakened by the exertions of the trip.

When John Tilley wrote again that Cecilia was failing fast, no one expected Frances Trollope, now in her seventieth year, to make the long hazardous trip across revolution-torn Europe to see her daughter. But by the spring of 1849 she had boarded the railroad and arrived in time to nurse once more one of her own who was dying. In spite of having recently seen Cecilia, and probably suspecting the truth of her condition, the death came, as she told Tom, as a "tremendous shock." Older and frailer now, she lost weight herself and found sleep impossible. Still, she rallied in her old manner, telling Tom, "I will do the best I can to get over it." Strength was necessary, for she saw clearly that the grandchildren, inheriting their mother's health, were all in a dangerous state. As ever, she frankly faced the truth. "I cannot conceal from myself that the chances are against us."[30] And indeed, none of Cecilia's children would survive to adulthood. Giving up plans for a return to Italy, Mrs. Trollope set about nursing once again. She interrupted this sad work only with a series of quick visits to family and friends, whom she had not seen for years. Again, she turned to the proven wellsprings of her life for sustenance and renewal. She journeyed to Brighton to see the Garnetts and visited her brother Henry who had been ill. In July she went to Ireland to see Anthony and Rose at Mallow. Afterwards she saw her sister Mary at Bristol and relatives at Exeter. These visits cheered her and brought her back with renewed strength to the frail grandchildren and the bereaved John Tilley. But neither nursing nor visits stopped the writing. A new contract with Colburn for two novels to be produced in 1850 was balm during these long sad days. As she wrote Tom, "This will give me occupation during the dull season which is approaching. . . ."[31]

In a short time John Tilley remarried. On her deathbed Cecilia had extracted his promise to take as his wife her cousin Mary Anne Partington, who would mother her large young family. Once this marriage was arranged, Mrs. Trollope could safely depart. She had discovered how much she was missing Tom and his new wife Theodosia. She felt their separation to be "almost too painful." Their life together, now nearly forty years old, had been, in her words, "a more perfect harmony than is often found, I believe, in any connection in life."[32]

But she could not make a simple return to the old life. For one thing, Tom was now married, and his mother-in-law having recently died, some arrangements were needed to accommodate Theo's elderly father in whatever new household arrangements were to be made. Mrs. Trollope took the lead in offering him a place in their Florence residence. Overriding all problems and objections, she was anxious to make whatever financial and domestic compromises were necessary to smooth the way for a resumption of life together with Tom. In all these negotiations she was the prime mover and most congenial spirit. As she wrote Tom encouragingly, "Depend upon it, the more the thing is pushed on, the easier it will appear to you. In these first days, every one feels and knows that things are out of joint; and the putting them into shape again is quite as easily done in one form as another, if a firm masterhand be set to the work."[33] Even as in the old days, Frances Trollope's was to be that firm masterhand. By the end of 1849 they were all on their way to Italy once again.

The journey back proved difficult. Mrs. Trollope fell ill with bronchial attacks and stayed behind at Pau, a winter health resort, while Tom, Theo, and Mr. Garrow went ahead to look for a home which would accommodate all their various needs. Mrs. Trollope was thus alone when she received the sorrowful news of her brother Henry Milton's death. It was more than just the disappearance of another link to the past. Henry had handled all her English finances and negotiations, a task that now would fall to his son. She chafed at her solitary state and wrote complaining letters to Tom which she regretted as soon as they were dispatched. Of all life's trials, she could endure loneliness the least. Working on her latest novel, *Petticoat Government* (1850), provided the only solace. By the summer, however, all was ready, and Mrs. Trollope made the long journey to what would be her last home, beguiling the difficult traveling time by reading the novels of George Sand.

Once settled, she entered into her previous routine, playing whist, seeing Tom, and writing novels. This was the period of her most unconventional and ingenious heroines, and her daughter-in-law found, in at least one of these late, unusual portraits, "certain touches . . . which, are copied from the life."[34] With her outward life firmly and regularly established she seemed ready to look within herself at the phenomenon of womanhood, what it had done and what it could do. All her late novels, in some respect or another, present the dominant, often beleaguered, but ultimately successful woman on her own.

In 1852 there were more changes. Theo was pregnant—and Anthony wrote humorous congratulations to Tom upon his impending fatherhood: "I am glad you are to have a child. One wants someone to exercise unlimited authority over as one gets old and cross." Anthony's life was increasingly prosperous and happy. A responsible employee of the Post Office, father of two boys, and persistently productive novelist whose works had received small but favorable notices and comparisons with his mother's works, Anthony was amazed at his own modest successes. He wrote his mother, "It often strikes me how wonderfully well I have fallen on my feet." When Tom's daughter Beatrice was born, the Anthony Trollopes came to Florence to see her (April 1853). Rose Trollope was obviously dazzled by her famous mother-in-law and described her as "the most charming old lady who ever existed." Mrs. Trollope took Rose all around the city, bought her an expensive silk dress, and presented her with a Roman mosaic brooch, a gift from Princess Metternich. Rose found her husband's mother totally unaffected by her fame and still rather unconventional, though worlds apart, despite her independent life, from "the Emancipated female" of the day. Her assessment of Frances Trollope was high compliment: "I do not think she had a mean thought in her composition."[35] Two years later, in 1855, when Frances again met Anthony and Rose, this time in Venice, she was still taking active walks on the sands of the Lido and obviously enjoying life.

Afterwards, Mrs. Trollope went through the Brenner Pass to Innsbruck, and on to London where she met David Hume, a well-known medium. Through him, she was attracted to mesmerism and, uncharacteristically, the world of departed spirits. This interest in the life beyond death was the first step in a slow decline which became more marked in the ensuing years. Hume followed Mrs. Trollope back to Italy and by the autumn of 1855 was a regular guest at the Villino Trollope. There, under his leadership, tables moved, chairs rocked, and handkerchiefs were found mysteriously tied in knots on certain evenings when guests gathered for seances. Now Mrs. Trollope looked to the past and consorted with the spirits of her father and her dead children. But her novel-writing—which continued for another year—still kept her tied to the realities of this world. Her last novel, *Town and Country* (her 35th), appeared in 1856. In 1857, however, when Anthony and Rose came again to Florence, she announced that she had "given up her pen," telling Anthony she was pleased "that her labours should be at an end, and that [his] should be beginning in the same field."[36]

Indeed, Frances Trollope must have taken great pride in the way her two surviving children were entering a profession she had so long and prolifically occupied. Tom was writing historical romances (he published *The Girlhood of Catherine de Medici* in 1856), and that same year Anthony completed *Barchester Towers,* the first of a series of novels which, in their fine observation of everyday English life, were extensions of his mother's talents at their highest. He was traveling too, to the West Indies in 1858 on Post Office business, and writing travel books on his experiences in the best tradition of Frances Trollope. Clearly, her literary posterity was already safe in the hands of her sons.

As her indulgence in memories of the past intensified, she slipped quietly into what is commonly called senility. It was in her case a gradual leave-taking from a long and rigorous life. She still walked daily, but now only in the garden and the open loggia. Cared for by the faithful Tom, the last years of her life were peaceful. She who had struggled and suffered so courageously died quietly on 6 October 1863, aged 84 years. In her last words, she was already with the tragic Tilleys who had departed before her. "Poor Cecilia," she was reported to say. It was perfectly in character that, even at the last, her compassionate thoughts were of her children.

Though many had criticized her and her works, she had never flinched either in truthfulness to her subjects or in devotion to those for whose support she wrote. Once, at a dinner party in London among the poets and literary luminaries, the critic Samuel Rogers turned to her, unaware of her identity, and observed, "They told me Mrs. Trollope was to be here. She has written a great deal of rubbish, hasn't she?" Without a moment's hesitation, she replied, "Well, she has made it answer."[37] Later, she repeated the story to others "with great glee." She had indeed made her work answer. With her talents, she had saved and supported her family and found the satisfaction of a productive personal life, making the double rhythm a source of energy to the end.

Chapter Two
The Travel Books

To be a lady traveler in the early part of the nineteenth century required certain unusual qualities of character: independence, toughness of spirit, and a willingness to move intrepidly in a world often uncharted by guidebooks or timetables. In Trollope's case, her entry into this somewhat unconventional field of female action came first because of the pressure of circumstances. But attracted by the financial and literary successes of her travel account of America, she quickly made plans for another book, this time about Germany, requiring, of course, another trip. Beyond the economic needs of her family, the impulse of travel was for Frances Trollope a move away from the domestic routine of her life. Her decision to become a traveler arose from a growing desire to be freer and to forge greater self-reliance. While the desire to travel came to her somewhat late in life, she still accomplished much in the field. In the first ten years of her writing career she made six major tours and composed travel accounts of each: *Domestic Manners of the Americans* (1832); *Belgium and Western Germany in 1833* (1834); *Paris and the Parisians in 1835* (1836); *Vienna and the Austrians* (1838); and *A Visit to Italy* (1842). Concurrently, she also wrote thirteen novels, several of them among the best she ever published. Obviously, the experience and movement of travel was invigorating to her artistic energies.

Six journeys in ten years had their effect on the personality and writing style of Frances Trollope. All were made without her husband, although she always went accompanied by some of her children and, later, always her son Tom. These journeys moved her further and further from the period stereotype of the angel in the house and made her resemble more the male adventurer off on his travels. While at home, she might be dominated by her family's needs, but on the road she created spans of time over which she had absolute control. Traveling also taught her habits of observation and careful note-taking which influenced her predominantly realistic approach to fiction. Travel uprooted her, made her less insular, more aware of new subjects like slavery, more sensitive to the situation of women, as she observed their lives in different countries.

One of the reasons she was able to break away from the narrow limits of women's lives in those days was her experience and success in the travel-book genre. Indeed, when one surveys the many contributions of women to this genre, from Isabella Bird's *Six Months in the Sandwich Isles* (1876) to Kate Marsden's *On Sledge and Horseback to Outcast Siberian Lepers* (1892), the sometimes seemingly lowly travel book assumes added importance as a vehicle for the emancipation of women in the nineteenth century.

All Trollope's travel books were informal and experimental in nature, the stress ever on people, not places. Their titles give clues to their fundamental essence: "Domestic Manners" in America; Paris, but also "the Parisians"; Austria, but also "the Austrians." In two, she included in the title the current date, thus emphasizing immediacy of subject matter and tone. All were "visits," not historical analyses, nor geographical compendia of information. They were the impressions of a sharp-eyed outsider of a specific segment of intensely realized time.

Taken together, more than the many novels she wrote, more than her peripheral fame as Anthony Trollope's mother, her travels and traveling accounts have been the source of her most enduring fame to date.

Domestic Manners of the Americans (1832)

Domestic Manners of the Americans, Trollope's first book, quickly made the author's fame and fortunes. Controversial from the first, it was vilified by the Americans, who saw it as slanderous revenge, precipitated by her failed Cincinnati Bazaar. In England the book fueled the then-current controversy over the extension of the suffrage (the Reform Bill of 1832) and was cited by both liberals and conservatives, who saw in the newly created American republic the clear results of democratic principles. The discussions were heated and sufficiently publicized to make the book a best seller and its author the "lion" of the current social season. As Trollope told her son Tom, "the Countess of Morley told me she was certain that if I drove through London proclaiming who I was, I should have the horses taken off and be drawn in triumph from one end of town to the other!"[1]

The book that occasioned all this furor and attention is a many-faceted narrative of the author's travels in America. Its overall framework is chronological and follows Frances Trollope's gradual transformation from daring adventurer, to beleaguered resident, to observant, note-taking tourist and author. Everything about the book was original, from its lively, colloquial style and large quantity of dramatic anecdote and dialogue, to Hervieu's unusual drawings of American manners in the style of novel illustrations rather than the scenic views then prevailing in travel books, to its concentration on a number of unifying and provocative themes, then highly charged with emotion. The opinions and voice of the author on these issues permeate the whole. Trollope speaks on political topics, like the American system of government versus the English; on social-domestic subjects, the casual me-first attitude of American life made visible in rude postures or repulsive customs like spitting; she takes religious stances, reviewing the effects of a secular state versus one with an established religion; and finally, delineates her views on the role and behavior of women in American life. Running alongside all of these was the book's most immediate source of contemporary interest, the author's constant counterpoint of comparison between England and America.

But there was yet another ingredient in the book's originality—its technique of direct reporting, an almost documentary approach to scene and character, with passage after passage in which the author lets people speak for themselves, with little or no background comment. The reader follows a Philadelphia lady through her daily activities, overhears a random conversation on a steamboat, and is lectured by a "literary gentleman" who claims that Shakespeare is obscene and Chaucer has had his day. These hundreds of dramatized slices of life are the source of the book's most lasting appeal.

The narrative line of *Domestic Manners* falls roughly into three parts, each having a distinctive subject matter and style. The first section is an adventure story, the account by a lone female of her travels in wild territory. The second contains Trollope's account of a two and a half year-long residence at Cincinnati. This section, with its intimate domestic detail, anecdotes, and recorded conversations, is the most historically famous and vital part of the book. The third narrative thread, which takes up after the Trollopes leave Cincinnati, is a more conventional traveler's account of a tour through the mid-Atlantic portions of the United States.

The adventure narrative of *Domestic Manners* (Chapters 1 to 3) is its shortest element, characterized by an emphasis on the description of exotic landscape and a pervasive sense of strangeness. Amid the mudbanks of the Mississippi, monstrous bulrushes, the floating debris of upended driftwood, and even "now and then a huge crocodile luxuriating in the slime" (1),[2] Frances Trollope and her party approach American territory. Spanish moss has converted all the trees to weeping willows, while everywhere burgeons the palmetto, the pawpaw, and countless varieties of ivied vine. As if America were an enchanted land, oranges, green peas, and peppers are miraculously growing outside, though it is Christmas time (2). In New Orleans the English lady traveler moves with wonder among blacks, graceful and elegant quadroons, and groups of wild and savage-looking Indians (2). In this section she draws her characters not as individuals, but as types, as amazing as the lush vegetation or as America's own tall tales. The Kentucky flatboat men, large and handsome, vault over the sides in colossean strides. To her, they seem inhabitants of another world, "a very noble-looking race of men" (3), of the same heroic dimensions as stories of a crocodile who had mauled in relentless and bloody succession a wife and five young children while the horrified father watched helpless (3). She narrates her trip up river as a mysterious journey into the heart of a region "condemned of nature," observing at the same time the wasteful if remarkably efficient American way of clearing the forests for farming. She renders the scene as nightmare: "the lurid glare of a burning forest was almost constantly visible" (3). For a while her eye was fascinated by the scenery, its vastness, and the "ceaseless continuity of the forest," but increasingly she turns to observe the rude and taciturn Americans who are her steamboat companions, their oaths, their crude eating habits, their incessant spitting, their disregard of women, and deliberate separation from "gentler companions" at dinner. Despite the magnificence of the landscape, she confesses that it was becoming "impossible not to feel repugnance to many of the novelties that now surrounded me" (3). Once her eye fell firmly upon the oddities of American social life, the adventure narrative was already receding into the background, and people, not landscape, became the major focus of her attention.

The highlight of the adventure section is her trip to Nashoba, which was, to her chagrin, only a primitive clearing in the forest which "rears its dark wall, and seems to say to man, 'so far shalt

thou come, and no farther!' " Through territory "wilder at every
step," the Trollopes pass tottering tree-trunk bridges and high trees
with "pendant vine branches." The "gay-plumaged" green parrots
made them feel they "were in a new world." There was trouble—
rain, flooding, and delay in "the novel wildness of the dark forest,"
and then the sudden sight of Nashoba, when Trollope sinkingly
realized her terrible mistake. "Desolation was the only feeling, the
only word that presented itself" (3). After only the most cursory
description of the Nashoba settlement, which by its briefness disguised the role Frances Wright and this utopian colony had played
in her decision to come to America, Frances Trollope abruptly brings
her readers out of the adventure narrative. Sailing up river for Mem-
phis, and then Cincinnati, she begins a thirty-month domestic so-
journ in America's heartland, which is the central and most important
section in her book.

In her Cincinnati chapters Trollope draws a devastating portrait
of a nineteenth-century American Middletown, a place where graz-
ing hogs clear the streets of refuse, where the gentleman "spit, talk
of elections and the price of produce, and spit again" (6), and where
the liveliest amusement is the Owen-Campbell debate on the evi-
dences of Christianity. It is "a triste little town," whose theater is
poorly attended, but whose chapels and revival meetings are packed
with women seeking activity and importance. Architectually, she
found it undistinguished, "but a little town, about the size of
Salisbury, without even an attempt at beauty in any of its edifices"
(4). It was laid out "in squares" with Gradgrindian regularity. Only
the pretty hills and forests around relieved the dreadful monotony
of simple life in Western America. Trollope's portrait of the "Athens
of the West" was not a flattering one.

In this section her approach resembles that recently taken by the
documentary film maker. After briefly sketching in the environment, she turned the camera eye on the Americans themselves,
letting them speak, act, and gesture. In and around her pictures
runs a texture of intermittent commentary and generalization on
American traits, practices, scenes, occupations, and activities. But
the important thing is the camera eye, the instrument of those
moments of revelation in which the American character was laid
bare in its most essential aspect. A steady stream of small epiphanies
forms the thematic logic of the Cincinnati section.

Structuring these pages further is a lightly sketched narrative line which begins on 10 February 1828, when the Trollopes reached Cincinnati and established residence there, and continues through their eventual settlement in a house in the country where they await Mr. Trollope and Tom, who arrived with the necessary funds for the building of the bazaar, an event which is mentioned only in the barest outlines. There are accounts of rural excursions, trips to see the shaking Quakers, camp meetings, and other local events. Then, when the "Cincinnati speculation" failed, the Trollopes departed in March 1830. This narrative framework preserves the reader's interest and allows Trollope to discuss a number of topics without losing the sense of immersion in daily experience.

Trollope found American life unattractive. Its outward forms and practices, stemming as they did from an egalitarian political system and philosophy, seemed, by European standards, mannerless and even downright rude. Without either elegance, or even propriety, Americans seemed to her to demonstrate a "total and universal want of manners, both in males and in females" (5). Spitting was the most prominant and palpable epitome of this American disregard for the graces and amenities of life, as were the almost deliberately rude postures men assumed in public places, especially the theater, "heels thrown higher than the head, the entire rear of the person presented to the audience"(13).

People who behaved so inconsiderately were not really sociable, even to one another. As each man concentrated on his own steady rise upwards, the American character turned in upon itself. When Trollope visited one farmer's wife, the woman professed herself unused to company and sociability. "I expect the sun may rise and set a hundred times before I shall see another human that does not belong to the family." About their consolation for such alienation Trollope is bitter and satiric: "But then they pay neither taxes nor tythes, are never expected to pull off a hat or to make a curtsey, and will live and die without hearing or uttering the dreadful words, 'God save the King' " (5).

Americans had little reverence for even their own leaders. When President Jackson arrived at Cincinnati, en route to Washington, his treatment by onlookers struck a characteristic note. Amid generally "cold silence," a gathered crowd commented openly and crudely on the recent loss of his wife. Trollope reproduced the dialogue of a "greasy fellow" who accosted Jackson thus:

"General Jackson, I guess?"

The general bowed assent.

"Why, they told me you was dead."

"No! Providence has hitherto preserved my life."

"And is your wife alive too?"

The general, apparently much hurt, signified the contrary upon which the courtier concluded his harangue by saying,

"Ay, I thought it was the one or t'other of ye." (13)

Thus, even the highest in the land was exposed to this "brutal familiarity," which Trollope believed was so characteristic of American manners.

She found Americans uninterested in the unprofitable amenities of life, "money-grubbing" people, whose primary concern was becoming prosperous. Material success was their main duty. "Every bee in the hive is actively employed in search of that honey of Hybla, vulgarly called money; neither art, science, learning, nor pleasure, can seduce them from its pursuit" (5). Trollope noted the consequent lack of attention to the role of leisure in American life. Indeed, Americans would develop an extensive concept of leisure only when it became a marketable commodity.

In the realm of art Americans exhibited a defensive insularity. Here again, Trollope lets her dramatic examples make the point. A gentleman of Cincinnati, "having a drawing put into his hands representing Hebe and the bird umquhile, sacred to Jupiter, demanded 'What is this?' 'Hebe,' replied the alarmed collector [confused by the similarity between the represented object and the American national symbol]. 'Hebe,' sneered the man of taste. 'What the devil has Hebe to do with the American eagle?" (7). A lady at a party advised "If you want to know what a beautiful city is, look at Philadelphia. . . . It is better worth talking about than that great overgrown collection of nasty, filthy, dirty streets, that they call London" (14). Through an extensive collection of such statements Frances Trollope revealed the inadequacies and compensatory postures of the new American republic in aesthetic matters.

Like many travelers, Trollope examined in closer detail those subjects that were most important to her. The role of women in America thus became a prominent topic in *Domestic Manners*. The Cincinnati section in particular, with its orientation in the domestic

sphere, presented the best opportunity for her to evaluate the lives
of American women. Indeed, hardly a chapter passes between 4 and
17 without some reference to women, whose situation in society
she epitomized in a harsh, pithy phrase: "lamentable insignificance."
While her remarks and pictured scenes are scattered across the whole
narrative, a coherent presentation of the American woman's life from
young womanhood to marriage does emerge from her pages.

Their spinsterhood was not usually long. American women married young and thus had little time for extensive education or other
mental development. As Trollope observes, "in no rank of life do
you meet with young women in that delightful period of existence
between childhood and marriage wherein, if only tolerably well
spent, so much useful information is gained, and the character takes
a sufficient degree of firmness to support with dignity the more
important parts of wife and mother" (12). And even for those who
had the means and opportunity to receive some training before
marriage, America's female educational institutions were inade-
quate. As Trollope somewhat sarcastically points out, "a 'quarter's'
mathematics, or 'two quarters' political economy, moral philosophy,
algebra, and quadratic equations, would seldom, I should think,
enable the teacher and the scholar, by their joint efforts, to lay in
such a stock of those sciences as would stand the wear and tear of
half a score of children and one help" (9).

Once married, the American woman's opportunities for personal
development dwindled still further. Although the degree of drudgery depended on social class, most women, Trollope observes, became domestic slaves or "teeming wives." This immersion in
household affairs she blamed on the lack of dependable servants.
Her frequent depictions of saucy and unruly young servant girls, so
often derided by her egalitarian critics, arose from Trollope's insight
that unless the married woman could rely upon domestic help in
organizing her family establishment, full self-development would
never occur.

Even in their leisure hours, as women sought to exit from their
limiting domestic sphere, they encountered further entrapment. At
evening parties they talked mainly to one another. Trollope depicts
many scenes in which women "herd together at one part of the
room, and the men at the other" (6). Conversation between the
sexes was awkward, given the radical differentiation of their daily
spheres of action. Thus, the separation of the sexes, obvious during

business hours, spilled over into social life, further isolating women in domestic enclosures, both spatial and temporal. Public events were also off female limits, like the lectures of the infamous Fanny Wright, or even theater or ballet. Women, Trollope notes, were "guarded by a seven-fold shield of habitual insignificance" (7).

But Cincinnati society could boast at least one exemplary young woman, the educated Emaline Flint, "the companion and efficient assistant of her father's literary labours." Frances Trollope's description concludes with the question toward which all her words on women had been leading: "Is it to be imagined that if 50 modifications of this charming young woman were to be met at a party, the men would dare to enter it reeking with whiskey, their lips blackened with tobacco, and convinced . . . that women were made for no other purpose than to fabricate sweetmeats and gingerbread, construct shirts, darn stockings, and become mothers of possible presidents? Assuredly not. Should the women of America ever discover what their power might be, and compare it with what it is, much improvement might be hoped for" (26). To Trollope, the moral and social tone of the new republic could only be improved by a greater participation of women in forming the domestic manners of the Americans.

Only in religion did American women find "that degree of influential importance which, in the countries of Europe, is allowed them throughout all orders and ranks of society" (8). Trollope was amazed to see the women bedecked in their best ribbons and bonnets, crowding into chapels, churches, meetinghouses and outdoor camps, participating not in an established liturgical religion, but rather in a rough-and-tumble emotionalism which, in her view, only demeaned and excited its participants. Her many descriptions of women at revivals, dominated by their ministers, nervous about sexual matters and yet dangerously aroused by the evangelical atmosphere, was the dramatic background for Frances Trollope's conclusion: "I never saw or read, of any country where religion had so strong a hold upon the women, or a slighter hold upon the men" (8). Religion was obviously a vehicle, and an inappropriate one, for American women to gain self-importance.

In the Cincinnati section Trollope describes both an indoor revival in one of the principal Presbyterian churches, where women come to listen to preachers and to pray all day and "often for a considerable portion of the night," and the more dramatic outdoor camp meeting.

In the latter, she faithfully describes the preacher's "shrill voice of horror" and "impressive eloquence." "No image that fire, flame, brimstone, molten lead, or red hot pincers could supply, with flesh, nerves, and sinews quivering under them, was omitted." With perspiration streaming down his face, "his eyes rolled, his lips . . . covered with foam, and every feature had the deep expression of horror." The culmination came with repeated invitations to "come then . . . and we will make you see Jesus, the dear gentle Jesus. . . . But you must come to him! You must not be ashamed of him; we will make way for you; we will clear the bench for anxious sinners to sit upon. Come, then! Come to the anxious bench, and we will show you Jesus! Come! Come! Come!" (8). At this incantation, young girls, trembling, sighing, sobbing, groaning, seated themselves, amid violent cries and shrieks and "convulsive accents," calling out "Oh Lord, Oh Lord Jesus! Help me Jesus," while the ministers comforted them with "from time to time a mystic caress." In rendering these scenes Trollope insisted the events were representative of many. She concluded the discussion with a provocative question: "Did the men of America value their women as men ought to value their wives and daughters, would such scenes be permitted among them?" (8).

Such scenes, culminating in pointed rhetorical questions and sharp generalizations, made the Cincinnati section of *Domestic Manners* both unforgettable and controversial. Drawing vivid memories from her personal notebooks, Frances Trollope created graphic pictures of life in an egalitarian society on America's frontier and accurately reproduced both speech idioms and characteristic gestures for an English public curious about the Yankees across the water. More important, she took these disparate scenes and made them representative, drawing from them powerful generalizations about American life, many as true today as when she wrote them. As an astute observation of the ordinary domestic life of a people, the Cincinnati chapters of *Domestic Manners of the Americans* have not often been surpassed.

In March 1830 Frances Trollope and her party departed from Cincinnati and began a slow journey eastward. They intended to return to England, but until enough money could be earned by Hervieu or cajoled from Mr. Trollope, they could not afford the fare. On these travels Frances Trollope continued to compile notes for her projected volumes on America, now no longer as resident, but as tourist. As she wrote about the America east of Cincinnati, she continued to be unsparing in her accounts of the inconveniences and irritations of American life, now those particularly associated with travel—bad accommodations and food, unsuitable inns, uncongenial company. But aware as she always was of herself and her discomforts, she was never unwilling to talk to anyone, nor was any detail too small for her careful observation. In the third section of *Domestic Manners* many of her old themes carry over—her preoccupation with religion and with the role of women—and some new ones emerge, particularly a persistent habit of comparison between whatever she sees in America and things English. Also in this third phase of the narrative Trollope raises aesthetic and political issues and devotes a large amount of space to descriptions of scenery and landscape.

Her place descriptions in this section are not really remarkable. Whenever she moves quickly through an area, her ability to capture essentials is perhaps no greater than that of the average tourist. Wheeling, Virginia, she reports, is a flourishing town, but rather black with coal mining, and not beautiful, except for the Ohio River (17). Baltimore is a beautiful city with a handsome approach, full of stately monuments, cathedrals, and museums. The highlight of her description is a visit to an infant school there, which she finds impressive (19). Mount Vernon offers fine river scenery and associations with General Washington, that "truly great man" (20). One sentence is all she devotes to Albany, "the state capital of New York, [which] has some very handsome public buildings; there are also some curious relics of the old Dutch inhabitants" (32). She is impressed by the flora and fauna, and like many other nineteenth-century travelers, she records the variety of trees—cedars, tulip, plane, sumac, juniper, and oak (21), and spends many pages describing the picturesque Mohawk valley (33), the Hudson valley, with the perpendicular Palisades, Manhattan Island's "leafy coronet gemmed with villas," the New York Highlands, and Washington Irving's Sleepy Hollow (32). Repeatedly, her descriptions center around combinations of rocks, trees, and water in picturesque arrangements. These natural settings are her primary focus now, and her writing lacks the strong emotions and deeply felt experiences of the Cincinnati section. Only when she has stayed longer than a few days in a place, had the opportunity to talk to people, and have some adventures of her own do her passages revive with the life of earlier sections. In this general category of description Trollope's lengthiest rendition is of the greatest American natural wonder, Niagara Falls. Niagara was one place she believed her book must include to be successful. She approached the falls in "wonder, terror, delight" (33), in active search of sublime subject matter. For the description of Niagara she adopted a florid style which is not her best or most characteristic voice. In her rendition Niagara is a "mighty cauldron," a "stupendous cataract," which presents "an idea of irresistible power." To her, "a shadowy mystery hangs about it" (33). Repeatedly, she pushed language toward hyperbole: the "awful beauty," the "wondrous crescent," the "hundred silvery torrents," the "liquid emerald" water, the "fantastic wreaths," and finally, the "shadowy mist that veils the horrors of its crash below, constitute a scene almost too enormous in its features for man to look upon." She resorted to quotation: "Angels might tremble as they gazed," and to classical allusions: "What was that cavern of the winds of which we heard of old, compared to this? A mightier spirit than Aeolus reigns here." These "tremendous" worked-up scenes contrast unfavorably with others in her more characteristic, critical voice. Like many another artist, she was perhaps unaware that the scenes that to her were more commonplace—her Cincinnati experiences—would be the truly unique part of her book.

Once she left the Falls, she stayed a few days in Buffalo, which she found "queer-looking," all its buildings with "the appearance of having been run up in a hurry, though every thing has an air of great pretension; there are porticos, columns, domes, and colonnades, but all in wood. Everybody tells you there, as in all their other new-born towns, and everybody believes, that their improvement, and their progression, are more rapid, more wonderful, than the earth ever before witnessed; while to me, the only wonder is, how so many thousand, nay millions of persons, can be found, in the 19th century, who can be content so to live. Surely this country may be said to spread rather than to rise" (33). In this almost offhand comment Trollope hit upon some hard truths of American life. In a contentment with synthetic versions of the real in the interest of haste Americans "spread out" with little thought for the future, burned forests to clear the land, erected buildings they knew would not last, and were ready to move west when they tired of what they had created. This carelessness toward the earth and makeshift forms of building would remain American problems into the twentieth century.

The final section of *Domestic Manners* contains Trollope's most explicit criticisms of America's social and political flaws. While she did not engage in lengthy philosophical examinations of democracy and egalitarian principles, leaving this, she said, to more "experienced and philosophical travelers" like her predecessor in writing a travel book about the United States, Captain Hall (31), she described instead America's treatment of three underprivileged groups—Indians, black slaves, and women. In the delineation of these specific situations she found the key to America's fundamental flaws. Her discussion of the limited lives of women occurs throughout the book and indeed is a major unifying theme.[3] Her third section contains several short descriptions of Indians and slaves. For all these groups America's much-touted principles of equality had failed. The results were debased human relations, perverted religious and cultural norms, and a daily life that was ungraceful and even ugly.

Of the negotiations between the Indians and the American government, Trollope remarked pointedly, "If the American character may be judged by their conduct in this matter, they are most lamentably deficient in every feeling of honour and integrity." She found the American treachery toward "the unhappy Indians" evidence of "the contradictions in their principles and practice" (20). Later, when she visited Lake Cananadaigua in upstate New York, she noticed, next to the ubiquitous American hotel ("the white man's mushroom palace," [33]), a shed housing two Indians, whom she depicted with great sympathy and respect. One was "an aged man, whose venerable head in attitude and expression indicated the profoundest melancholy." The other was a youth, whose eyes contained "a quiet sadness." "There they stood, the native rightful lords of the fair land, looking out upon the lovely lake which yet bore the name their fathers had given it, watching the threatening storm that brooded there; a more fearful one had already burst over them" (33). When the Trollopes traveled, the gentle Indians received them with smiles, whereas the Americans were rude and aggressive. Once, when a "lady" shoved her way into their carriage places, helped by some rowdy whiskey drinkers, Trollope wondered "whether the invading white man, in chasing the poor Indians from their forests have done much towards civilizing the land." She answered her own question: "For myself, I almost prefer the indigenous manner to the exotic" (33). Certainly, the Indian culture seemed to provide material for the land's most authentic artistic expression. In Washington she found the architectural detail on the pillars of the Capitol—arrangements of ears and leaves of Indian corn—"the only instance . . . in which America has ventured to attempt national originality; the success is perfect" (20).

Her sympathy with the Indians went together with her position on slavery, a subject she would treat extensively in her novel *Jonathan Jefferson Whitlaw* (1836), in which she also included favorable scenes of Indians. Her experiences in America, especially her lengthy stay at Stonington, Virginia, with her family friend Anna Maria Garnett Stone, persuaded Trollope that slavery constituted the great central flaw at the heart of the American system of government and society:

The same man who beards his wealthier and more educated neighbor with the bullying boast, "I'm as good as you," turns to his slave, and knocks him down, if the furrow he has ploughed, or the log he has felled, please not this stickler for equality. There is a glaring falsehood on the very surface of such a man's principles that is revolting. (22)

In Virginia it was illegal to teach a slave to read, and "this law speaks volumes." While domestic slaves generally were well cared for, "they may be sent to the South and sold," and the southern plantations were "the terror of American negroes." One man, who heard such was to be his fate, Trollope reported, "sharpened the hatchet with which he had been felling timber, and with his right hand severed his left from the wrist" (22). Referring the reader to what she termed Captain Hall's judicious and abler treatment of the subject, Trollope composed dramatic scenes far superior to any of Hall's abstract discussions of slavery.

Her stories are unforgettable illustrations of the way in which "the greatest and best feelings of the human heart were paralyzed by the relative positions of slave and owner." In one, a young female slave, about eight years old, had eaten a biscuit "temptingly buttered" but "copiously sprinkled with arsenic for the destruction of rats." When Frances Trollope saw the situation, she prepared an emetic and administered it. A young white girl, astonished and repelled by this instinctive action, exclaimed: "My! If Mrs. Trollope has not taken her in her lap, and wiped her nasty mouth! Why I would not have touched her mouth for 200 dollars" (22). Trollope rendered the story in great detail and added considerable commentary. For her it epitomized the way in which American whites did not see the black as a fellow human being. Here, as in the Cincinnati section, she again becomes the documentary reporter, turning the camera upon the subject that unconsciously reveals the truth of the American character in a brief pictured moment.

Trollope was not complimentary in her final evaluation of American society. As she begins her summation, she notes: "I suspect that what I have written will make it evident that I do not like America" (34). While she recognized America's beauty and abundance, Trollope's prevailing judgment is negative, based on three objections: First, in this book so full of diverse American characters, she confesses, of the people, "I do not like them. I do not like their principles, I do not like their manners, I do not like their opinions" (34). Second, she does not like their system of government. In a fanciful depiction of its formation she wrote:

Their elders drew together, and said, "Let us make a government that shall suit us all; let it be rude, and rough, and noisy; let it not affect either dignity, glory, or splendour; let it interfere with no man's will, nor meddle with any man's business . . . let every man have a hand in making the laws, and no man be troubled about keeping them." (34)

Finally, Trollope protests the tyranny and insularity of Americans with regard to strangers. Americans will not accept criticism, for they believe "they are the first and best of the human race, that nothing is to be learnt, but what they are able to teach, and that nothing is worth having, which they do not possess" (34).

Despite the serious problems she had identified, Trollope, however, still believed that a remedy could be found. Greater tolerance for diversity and reform of domestic manners, brought about through the agency of women could, she suggested, smooth the rough edges and help remove the hypocrisies which flawed this first democratic republic. Should the Americans ever learn the graces, refinements, "the chivalry of life," they would become "one of the finest countries on the earth" (34). Her own long experience in the heartland of this new country had given her, however, little enthusiasm or optimism about such predictions.

The Refugee in America (1833)

Before the next year was over Trollope made further use of her American materials in a first novel, *The Refugee in America*. As she told her friend Julia Pertz, she still had a reservoir of "good yankee stories" which could be used in a work of fiction. And indeed, she was one of the first writers of her age to discover how the experiences of travel could be turned into material for a novel. Later Charles Dickens would follow her lead, using his American experiences to bolster the sagging sales of *Martin Chuzzlewit,* and her son Anthony and many subsequent novelists would learn how to mine this rich resource.[4]

In terms of its plot, *The Refugee* is pure melodrama, complete with smugglers and fugitives. A young nobleman, Lord Darcy, is accused of a stabbing murder of which he is innocent. Mr. Gordon, an old friend of Darcy's mother, and his daughter Caroline, befriend the fugitive. In disguise, Darcy accompanies the Gordons to America, where he hides while trying to clear his name. Trollope added to these stock materials a whole gallery of diverse American characters to make of her novel something different. An evil relative, now in America, conspires to murder Darcy, but fails. Later, Darcy returns to England where his innocence is finally established. The criminals are apprehended; Darcy marries an American girl who is, after some hesitation, welcomed into the noble family, and all ends happily for the Darcys and Gordons back in England.

As might be expected in a first novel, the narrative line often lacked real direction and was marred by a number of implausible events. Still, when Trollope propelled her characters through places and situations she herself had experienced, the book came to life; it sold well with the reading public, despite poor reviews from the professional critics. Indeed, much of the material of *The Refugee* is simply *Domestic Manners* warmed over. First, there is the similarity of settings. Trollope took her characters over much the same route that she had traveled in eastern America. The party goes from New York to Rochester, to the Genesee Falls, Niagara, and then Washington. In several cases, like the description of Lockport, strong verbal similarities support the conjecture that her travel book was open beside her as she wrote the novel.[5]

While it appears that the constant shifting of scene is demanded by the exigencies of the plot, as the Gordons and the refugee flee

their pursuers, in reality Trollope was only capitalizing on her materials. Thus, a visit to Niagara Falls provides not only the occasion
for an exciting attempt on Darcy's life, but allows the author some
more "sublime" raptures on the falls. When the Gordons visit the
hearthside of Squire Burns, Trollope writes a genre scene straight
from the pages of *Domestic Manners*. The setting recalls Nashoba:
"The log hut, divided by an open portico into two separate dwellings; the tall stalks of Indian corn, waving their tassels in the breeze
of the night; the dark impenetrable wall of forest, that seemed to
form the only fence and barrier to the cleared space around him;
the various sized, and long handled gourds lying about for household
purposes; the loud, deep, unceasing croak of the bull-frog, and at
intervals, the hollow, painful howl of the distant wolf, all spoke of
a country that was not his own." The characters too would be familiar
to readers of her first book: Burns offers hospitality in the form of
johnnycakes, venison, and hominy, and the children have the elaborate names Americans liked to give their offspring: Benjamin
Franklin, Ophelia, Euphrosyne, and Monroe. The mother is active,
though sickly looking, and the narrator concludes the scene with
the comment: "The mistress of the house looked ill, and overworked,
and had not the children called her mother, might have been taken
for their grandmother."[6]

She also crowded into the novel many of her earlier observations
of American traits, as well as her by now well-known prejudices.
In the novel the English are amazed by the lack of conversation at
dinner, by the absence of books, prints, pianos, cards, or chess
games in the drawing rooms, and horrified by American reading
habits, all of which she had strongly criticized in *Domestic Manners*.[7]

Because Trollope liked (and apparently believed) American tall
tales, she reused the story of Sam Patch and his incredible bear who
performed aerial feats and dove together off factory roofs, bridges,
and the Genesee Falls. Later Mark Twain complained that Trollope
had been hoaxed by these and other stories (such as the man-eating
crocodile in the Mississippi): "Unfortunate tourists! People hum-
bugged them with stupid and silly lies, and then laughed at them
for believing and printing the same."[8] That she was gullible may
be true; her cleverness lay in the way she used such stories with
dramatic effect and captured the interest of her readers with such
extraordinary details of local color.

In *Domestic Manners* Trollope had recorded conversations between Yankees in which questions are answered only with more questions, with no one receiving any useful information. In *The Refugee* a New Englander successfully dodges questions about Lord Darcy: "the triumphant Yankee rubbed his hands, and thanked the Lord that he was not like other men, to let out his secrets in that fashion." Trollope's views of American literary soirées also reappear in the novel, and the average American seems as foolish and prejudiced about women as he had been in reality.[9] Mr.Gordon asks Caroline to join some gentlemen conversing on the advantages and peculiarities of the United States, but when the ladies arrive, the conversation lags. "The gentlemen were, as Mr. Gordon had described them, well-informed and agreeable; but as to bringing any intellect into a discourse with ladies, that was quite out of the question" (2:127).[10] As the narrative progresses, the old observations are resurrected and incorporated intact in the novel.

The Refugee presents a gallery of American stereotypes. The Gordons' guide is a calculating miser who must be paid extra for every service he renders. His speech is salted with samples from Trollope's list of Americanisms: "I calculate—an ugly fix—tolerable 'cute—right straight." Squire Burns is the boastful American who believes the English secretly envy America. Mrs. Fidkin is a patriot, whose whole purpose in life is to proclaim the superiority of American womanhood. The Gordons' landlady is a Yankee who overcharges her renters whenever possible. Miss Fidkin is the "accomplished" female, with more "quarters" in the arts and sciences than any other young woman in the company (1:19, 30–32, 89 ff., 119).

Several characters are closely modeled on the author's own experiences. The story of the de Clairvilles parallels that of Frances Trollope and Auguste Hervieu at Nashoba. When the de Clairvilles arrive and are astonished at the primitive state of the Utopian colony "Perfect Bliss," their reaction recalls that of Hervieu, as described by Trollope's letter from Nashoba. "I think I never saw a man in such a rage. He wept with passion and grief mixed." Although Hervieu lived on to become her illustrator, Trollope has her fictional de Clairville die of a broken heart.[11]

Although the book contains some favorable American characters, they are always clear about the basic superiority of the English. One of them even puts off a proposed trip to England because he fears the comparison might be too painful. Emily Williams, the American heroine, is captivated by the English visitors, all of whom speak with such polish that she can find their like only in the pocket volume of Shakespeare which she surreptitiously reads. Caroline Gordon, a blossoming reformer, tutors Emily in proper English; immediately, Emily begins to confuse "learn" and "teach" and burgeons forth with all manner of atrocious Americanisms. A page or two later and all is well; Emily is a quick and convenient pupil. Trollope's point is clumsily made here. Still, the logic of the narrative must have been comforting. Her American girl is quickly transformed, brought back to England, and safely married to the English lord.

In each of her subsequent novels of American life a surrogate Frances Trollope appears. In *The Refugee* and later *The Old World and the New* (1849) the character is a refined, intellectual, and critical Englishwoman who goes abroad. In *The Barnabys in America* she is a dynamic, unconventional middle-aged vulgarian. In this first appearance Caroline Gordon is the mouthpiece for the author's objections to America. Examples abound. Caroline protests the lack of gaiety in the people: "I have never heard a hearty laugh since I entered the country." It is Miss Gordon who asks: "Will you tell me how you reconcile your theory of freedom with the condition of your negroes? or your treatment of the Indians with your doctrine of equal rights?" Caroline even begins "collecting attitudes for her book of sketches on the American graces," surely echoing the woman who went home and reported on America a few years before. [12]

The genesis of the idea for a love interest between a cultivated English man and a free-spirited American originates in *The Refugee* and is repeated in *The Barnabys in America.* Later Anthony Trollope picked it up masterfully in *The Way We Live Now* (1875), *He Knew He Was Right* (1869), and *The Duke's Children* (1880). The pattern then passed to Henry James, who remarked on the success of his British fellow-novelist in a field soon to be his own: the depiction of the American female. "The American girl was destined, sooner or later, to make her appearance into British fiction, and Trollope's treatment of this complicated being is full of good humor and that fatherly indulgence, that almost motherly sympathy, which characterizes his attitude throughout toward the youthful feminine. He has not mastered all the springs of her delicate organism nor sounded all the mysteries of her conversation." [13] But the start of this theme belonged to Frances Trollope. To be sure, she did not explore all its possibilities. Usually, the girl, as in *The Refugee,* is too quickly brought round to see that English ways are superior. Frances Trollope was interested in the situation only insofar as it provided a device permitting two people to debate the contrasts between American and English life. By adding a love interest to the debate, she kept her novel-reading public happy. But the device itself stems from *Domestic Manners,* with its host of questioning Americans and their endless catechism whose purpose is always to prove that the American way of life excels. Often stilted and heavily weighted to favor the English side, the situation was nevertheless original, amusing, and popular. Frances Trollope's instinct about the English appetite for American subject matter was correct. *The Refugee,* for all its flaws, was not a disappointing first novel; the first edition sold out almost immediately. These two books on America established her reputation and launched her writing career.

Belgium and Western Germany (1834)

With the earnings from her American books and her experimental Gothic potboiler *The Abbess* (1833), Trollope began to plan for another trip to write another book, this time on Germany. She wrote her friend Julia Garnett Pertz, who lived in Hanover, that she was ready to "start for some watering place on the Rhine with the commission to *make a book.*" She could not indulge in a lengthy visit with her friend for, as she explained, "I *must* be ready with my book by November and as yet I have merely notes."[14]

Trollope was hoping to capitalize on her own recent successes, as well as on the current vogue in travel books. Indeed, in *Belgium and Western Germany,* one of her first big scenes was a visit to the battlefield at Waterloo, where the setting recalled the high adventures of that famous encounter, "the battered walls, the dismantled and fire-stained chapel . . . the traces of attack upon attack, still renewed and still resisted" which "bring the whole scene before one with tremendous force" (1:89). Trollope dramatically brought imagined scenes to life. "I fancied I saw [the victorious generals] surrounded by their staff, waiting with trembling eagerness to learn who among their brave companions still lived to share their triumph" (1:90). The field itself seemed so "awful" that "no great stretch of imagination seemed necessary to people it," although "a poet might easily have fancied that the air was darkened by the waving banners of a spectre host careening over it" (1:91). She was, however, equally alive to the way modern society was exploiting interest in such places to make the spot a tourist trap. "A mile before we reached the ground, we were addressed on each side of the carriage by men who offered to be our guides over it: women, too, with baskets on their arms containing relics of the battle, came offering imperial eagles, bullets, and brass buttons for sale" (1:83 ff.).

She was not alone in her attention to the subject of travel or in her interest in Germany. In the same year that *Belgium and Western Germany* appeared eight other travel books described this same area. [15] The world was becoming an easier place to get around in; the number of tourists and tours was increasing, and the number of travel books was growing too. By now certain specific types of the genre had already established themselves in the public mind. Some were pleasure tours, whose titles ("light sketches," "airy nothings") indicated the end and aim of their authors. Others were books about remote parts of the earth, whose strangeness was their main appeal. Some were guidebooks for the increasingly peripatetic average Englishman. Others were more serious works, giving views of political and religious topics, more often directed at reforming English institutions than to describing foreign places. As the number of such books grew, readers began to look more closely at the abilities and acquirements of the traveler and his or her personality, thus subtly shifting the focus of attention from subject matter to style. The author's genius and peculiarities, his habits of mind and manner of presentation, not the description of landscape, became the central focus. In this increasingly crowded genre Trollope's distinctive voice and her growing abilities as a novelist made her books successful.

Over the next nine years she wrote four more travel books, all of them popular and several going into subsequent editions. In each, a strong and coherent authorial voice emerges. In *Domestic Manners* the disappointed liberal is disgusted with utopian or democratic experiments. In *Belgium and Western Germany* the conservative traveler admires the authoritarian King of Prussia and lectures the English reading public on the errors of the Great Reform Bill. In *Paris and the Parisians* (1836) the Tory Englishwoman deplores the disruptions of revolutions and supports Louis Phillipe, no rightful monarch, but at any rate, a king. In *Vienna and the Austrians* (1838) a bedazzled Frances Trollope hobnobs with Metternich and the social elite and praises Austrian absolutism. In *A Visit to Italy* (1842) she becomes a Virgilian guide to art treasures and the past. Whatever the subject, the reader never forgets the author's presence or her strong views about what she sees.

Another reason for Trollope's popularity as a writer of travels stemmed from her developing skills as an author of fiction. Indeed, because she was always writing a novel at the same time as she was compiling travel notes, her travel-book form merged with that of the novel. The events at hand and the evolving journey itself became her plot. The people she saw became mouthpieces of the ideas and social situations they represented, and she heightened them in almost Dickensian fashion. She made character prominent in a genre where place and exposition usually dominated. She knew how to use setting both as landscape and as a backdrop of social causation. Throughout, she treated opinions, ideas, and culture dramatically and creatively. Other fictional techniques enliven her travel books—digressions, catalogues, dialogues, set scenes. Her books had narrative structures, vivid characters, settings rich with the sights, sounds, and smells of everyday, and above all, a dominant world view. Her goal was not a colorless objectivity, and her style became, accordingly, a mixture of satire and the familiar personal essay. To her magpie instinct to collect facts, she now added a growing artistic ability to shape such facts into scenes that vibrated with life. With such credentials, and her natural courage and physical stamina, she was clearly qualified to embark upon the writing of travel books.

Like most of her others, her second travel account, *Belgium and Western Germany*, reveals a fundamentally conservative bias, even while it cannot be called primarily a political work. Yet her interest in the area arose from political considerations. In the summer of 1830 revolt had broken out in the United Netherlands. Rebels had proclaimed the independence of Belgium and drafted the most liberal constitution in all Europe. Later it would serve as a model for liberals everywhere during the upheavals of 1848. Trollope included in her book much adverse comment on the result of that revolution and praise for the authoritarian style of monarchy. At least in part her intention was to attack the liberal reforms then proceeding the England. She noted pointedly:

At home, I had of late been accustomed to hear every voice from the class, emphatically styled *the people,* whether heard through the medium of the press, or in listening to their conversation, expressive of contempt and dislike for their own country, its institutions, and its laws. . . . Far different is the state of public feeling in Germany. Ask a Prussian . . . his opinion of his country . . . and you will be answered by such a hymn of love and praise, as might teach those who have ears to hear, that passing a reform bill is not the most successful manner of securing the affection and applause of *the multitude.* (1:130–31)

Repeatedly, she used her observations of the German system to lecture the English public. "Where everyone knows his place, and keeps it," she wrote, "there can be no danger of jostling." Aware of the criticism that such remarks were sure to receive, she nevertheless defended the accuracy and seriousness of her conclusions:

It may be objected, to any opinion I may give as to the political feeling of Germany, that it is not in the course of a summer's tour, any important information on such a subject can be obtained. . . . Truth, however, is not the less true, because it is obvious. (2:218–20)

Throughout, her political message was clear: the Germanies should stand as lessons and models for England in their orderliness and political and social stability.

Still sensitive to the woman theme she had developed in *Domestic Manners,* she again included in her new book vignettes of the lives of women. She included the Journal of a Belgian Lady (given her by a friend, 1:111–14) and visited a convent of Belgian sisters, nuns who could be absolved from their vows, should they so choose. Trollope noted that few took advantage of this privilege, a fact she was quick to analyze. The women lived in comfort and freedom and had "quite a little town within their walls." Each had her own house, with its inhabitant's name over the door, and "altogether seem . . . to be of more consequence, each in her own circle, than they would have been had they retained their situations as individual single women, instead of becoming members of a large community" (1:40–42). She had, characteristically, nothing but praise for these self-sufficient, comfortable young women.

Much of what she saw in Germany, however, she idealized, as when she watched the female vine dressers "perched 300 feet above the river . . . without a thought of danger," or the peasant girl "cultivating her rich flower-bed, and singing the delicious strains of her country with taste and feeling . . . as refined a picture of rural life as we can hope to find anywhere, beyond the bounds of

Arcadia" (2:199–200 ff.). Lacking the intimate knowledge of her American years, she resorted to such romanticized portraits, to a provincial sketch of a Belgian lady (1:111), to details of external dress, as when she is struck in Antwerp by "the Spanish air of the women," with their "mantillas and concealment of face" (1:46). And while her observations were surely conscientious (she once coaxed the lady of the house at which she was staying "to exhibit the stays she wore on great occasions. They were unquestionably of many pounds weight; and were furnished on both sides with iron bars, which . . . must enter, if not into her soul, at least into her heart, every time she stooped" 1:12), she could not provide that analysis of society based on the condition of the female half of it which she did in her more comprehensive presentation of the position of women in America.

But while her conservative politics and interest in women remained constant, her angle of vision had radically altered. She who had lacked letters of introduction in America and lived as an outcast from polite society, now hobnobbed with the great. She called upon Her Royal Highness the Landgravine of Hesse-Homburg, who was a Princess of England, and was shown through her palace near Frankfurt. This distancing from the domestic manners of the people put Trollope at something of a disadvantage, as did her inability to speak German. Still, while she did not provide a broad compendium of information about life in Belgium and Western Germany, she knew how to make the most of the more limited scenes she saw.

With the novelist's instinct Trollope let people reveal themselves in skillfully managed speech and action, even while she pointed her dramatic stories toward more general truths. Her book abounds in vivid sketches of characteristic people. Some are brief: smoking gentlemen "with the stupifying pipe continually in their hands" (1:183–84); Jews at synagogue in Frankfurt, and the rabbi in a flat cap, who "twisted a white blanket, edged with blue, around him, and chanted from a large volume, in a most inconceivable variety of tones; bowing his head, as he did so, almost incessantly" (1:248). The radical students, their hair "long and exquisitely dishevelled; throats bare, with collars turned back almost to the shoulders," presented foreheads bared "à la Byron" and wild eyes "rolling à la Juan" (1:150). There were several longer descriptions of the gamblers at Baden and other pleasure spots, which, taken together, revealed

more about the current madness for gambling than the more ob-
jective, statistical accounts of some other travel books.[16]

Brave officers, whose blood never fell back upon their hearts when an
enemy faced them in the field, turn lividly pale at the sound of "Rouge
perd . . . couleur gagne"; and I have watched men whose eagle eye, and
proud demeanour, looked as if they could not quail before anything on
earth, shrink into littleness, as the gold they had madly thrown upon the
table was carelessly raked up by the callous bankers. . . . I have watched
it, till I have expected some ruined victim, mad with suffering, would
crush them to death beneath his feet. (2:69–71)

Such lines, more like scenes from a novel than a visit to a spa, are
among the most powerful sections of this book.[17]

Next to character development, the description of scenery occupies
an important place in her presentation of this picturesque area of
the world. Trollope depicts Charlemagne's Aix la Chapelle, Hei-
delberg's ruins, the "wildly picturesque" streams that descend from
the Black Forest to the Rhine. She sketches in the rich fields of
Flanders and the gardens of Schwetzingen, full of "terraces, foun-
tains, aviaries, temples, waterfalls, grottos, groves, parterres, lawns,
lakes, statues, mosques, baths, boats, and bridges" (1:283–84),
while trying hard to avoid, if possible, "the writing descriptions in
issimo" (1:294). She did not always achieve this goal, however, and
the book abounds with descriptions of castles, ruins, terraces, forests,
and gardens on the beautiful Rhine and the "pellucid" Neckar. As
she herself remarked, approaching Neckarsteinach, a lovely town
surrounded by towering rocks, the ruins of two stately castles, bright
green meadows around the river, boats, houses, and hanging gardens, "It was just such scenery as one longed to revel in" (1:300).
Scenery and people merged in Trollope's development of a new
source of material: the modern tourist on his travels. In an age just
discovering both the delights and drawbacks of tours for middle-
class travelers, Trollope turned a sharp eye on her fellow passengers.
With the advent of the steamboat and rapid overland carriage, many
seeking the grand tour experience passed too quickly through the
new lands they had come to see. In one steamboat ride she noted
some young ladies frantically sketching scenes that were soon out
of sight and some bustling young men trying to enjoy "the landscape
through an eye glass" (1:215). An innkeeper on a Rhine island
found himself without business, for the notion of a leisurely tour

seemed a thing of the past. Trollope herself thought Cologne needed two months, not two days, "but as long as steamboats keep running up the Rhine, the giddy throng . . . will never spare time to examine this interesting old city, with one tenth part of the attention it deserves" (1:136). On land, travel had accelerated. A lady in a diligence told Frances Trollope: "I and my nephews make a point of never stopping to look at things" (1:133).

For her own part, whenever she was forced to travel this way, she resented the need to keep up the pace. "The more beautiful the objects on every side, the more discontented I grow at being whisked past them" (2:149). The book became a plea for the old leisurely kind of travel as she repeatedly showed her readers the dangers of modern tourism, with its group arrangements, cheap souvenirs, and rapid impersonal transportation. At Marburg she failed to indulge a desire to explore the castle because "there stood the diligence, with the horses all ready, and the horn of the conductor at his mouth! and there stood I, inwardly vowing that I would never again chain myself in the same manner" (2:211). At the Protestant Church of St. Thomas she found the Count of Nassau and his daughter's remains "kept in glass cases and clothed in trumpery garments," exhibited "for a penny a-piece to all comers." In all that she found something "revoltingly indecent" (2:76–77). But speed was her most constant complaint, and she frequently wrote of "the vexation of being whirled past objects that you are longing to gaze upon" (1:56–57).

As the book approached its conclusion, in contrast to her hapless fellow tourists, Trollope emerged firmly as an ideal traveler. She took time, looked long, and explored fully the land she had come to see. Once, she even had herself locked inside a dungeon for half an hour (2:60), just to experience what imprisonment in a medieval castle was like. "I had read of the secret tribunal, its frightful cruelties, and its hidden strength, but here I was in the very midst of the fearful recesses" (2:39). Surely her readers relished this touch of the gothic, as did Trollope herself, who cheerfully recorded, while stepping into "this region of blackest night," that "I did not shrink from the undertaking" (2:61).

When she reached the Brocken, in the Harz Mountains, rich in associations with witches and devils, she saw the potential for "sublime" scenes as great as those she had penned about Niagara. But now she resisted the merely static presentations of landscape ("It is always dangerous to dwell in description upon any scene, the effect of which is greatly to excite the imagination" (2:229), and cast herself, instead, as the adventuring traveler with place as the backdrop. She ascended the Brocken on a mule, over rocks, through gigantic pines, amid rain and storm, across noisy torrents, into a "darker world" than even Dante could imagine, and spent the night on top in a small cabin. The main focus was Trollope's adventuring: she noted pointedly, "I was lost in admiration at my own undaunted courage" (2:246). The next day, in the middle of a raging storm, she made the descent strapped to the donkey. Despite breathlessness and even some fear, she experienced that "exaltation of spirits" that travel always aroused in her.

The book was fresh and genuine, and the critics praised her initiative and daring. "She was not satisfied to tread in the footsteps of the common tourist and to yield herself implicitly up to the guidance of an innkeeper, a *valet de place,* or a coachman. She sought out objects for herself, pursued the picturesque where it was likely to be found."[18] Soon she was writing her publisher with plans for yet another travel account: "Did circumstances permit, I should greatly like to scribble a little gossip on the present queer state of society in Paris."[19]

Indeed, she regarded herself now as a professional travel writer. Although she had published two novels to moderate success and completed another, she continued to view her travel books as her most important artistic activity. She was troubled by the delays attending the publication of her most recent novel only because it represented an important source of traveling funds. In a letter to her publisher she set forth the relationship between these two parts of her writing life:

Since I have felt it my duty to write, I have devoted such a portion of each day to the occupation, as would enable me to keep my place before the public. . . . Though my novels are read, my reputation must chiefly be sustained by traveling, and I love the occupation well enough to look forward with hope and pleasure to future excursions. I have been often told that I ought to visit Italy (Venice particularly) and Sicily—and I hope to be able to do so—but the truth is, that however well the public may like my traveling memoranda, the expenses incurred in collecting them are much too heavy to render the employment profitable, or even prudent. The publishing some work of imagination, written in the retirement of my quiet home, in the interval between my costly ramblings, is the only method by which I can enable myself to undertake them.[20]

As Trollope tried to maintain a balance between her traveling accounts and novels, the two genres came to have mutual influence upon each other. While fictional techniques came to dominate the travelogues, her novels also benefited from this cross-fertilization of types—from the *Refugee in America* and *Jonathan Jefferson Whitlaw*, through *The Barnabys in America, A Romance of Vienna,* and *The Robertses on Their Travels* to the work that concluded her writing career, *Fashionable Life: or Paris and London.* For Trollope, whose life seemed always to be filled by doing two things at a time, such artistic interaction proved stimulating and productive of original works.

Paris and the Parisians in 1835 (1836)

Whereas America and Germany had been new areas to Trollope, Paris was more familiar ground and had always been a favorite location, home of her friends the Garnetts, whom she had visited in 1823 when she produced one of her first writing efforts, a journal of a visit to La Grange, home of the much admired General Lafayette. And by now she was so accomplished a writer of travels that *The Spectator* suggested that *Paris and the Parisians* might be used to "deduce the laws of the craft" concerning travel books. Indeed, as the reviewer concluded, "to anybody who would wish to acquire the trade of book-making, *Paris and the Parisians* should be read, studied, and analyzed."[21]

For this book Trollope again employed the techniques of her fictional art; rather than writing straight expository prose, she used the device of letters home to a friend and cast much of her material as dialogues in which characters debate the relative merits of French and English social habits, modern French literature, the process of trial by jury, or the government of Louis Phillipe. Profuse catalogues of her observations and descriptive scenes, and light essays on current subjects alternated with those dramatic portions. Indeed, as one critic noted of the book: "All she writes is amusing, partly because of the originality of her own ideas, and partly because she has a curious way of illustrating the ideas of others."[22]

The most original part of the book is its structure, which reflected her judgment that Paris was a city of contradictions. Its surface was an air of "ceaseless jubilee" and "eternal holiday," which she described copiously (1).[23] Parisian people loved to bask in the open air and show the world their *joie de vivre*. "The bright, clear atmosphere seems made on purpose for them; and whoever laid out the boulevards, the quays, the gardens of Paris" knew how the citizens loved to assemble for shared pleasure (29). Sorrow and suffering seemed banished. "Everywhere else you see people looking anxious and busy at least . . . but here the glance of every eye is a gay one; and even though this may perhaps be only worn in the sunshine, and put on just as other people put on their hats and bonnets, the effect is delightfully cheering to the spirits of a wandering stranger" (70). Repeatedly she noted "that indescribable air of gayety which makes every sunshiny day look like a fête: the light hilarity of spirit . . . the cheerful tone of voice, the sparkling glances of the numberless bright eyes; the gardens, the flowers, the statues of Paris," taken together, produced "an effect very like enchantment" (6).

But Trollope's book also showed the grim side of urban Paris by means of a series of interpolated narratives, some about murders and suicides, another describing her own visit to the crowded Paris morgue ("I was steadfast in my will to visit it, and I have done it." [37]). In addition to her own stories, she summarizes the action of two violent plays by Victor Hugo, then playing to crowded audiences. By such imaginative and diverse means she projected the brutalities hidden behind the "delightful spectacle" Paris presented to the merely casual visitor.

She drew people in strong outlines, heightening their representative traits. The language of one critic emphasized the pictorial aspect of her art: "There is a brightness about her portraits . . . that at once fixes upon our memory."[24] Her subjects ranged from the famous (Madame Recamier, Mademoiselle Mars, Victor Hugo, George Sand) to prisoners and revolutionaries, some in conical crowned hats with "long matted locks that hang in heavy, ominous dirtiness" (24). Using talk and gestures, she brought brief sketches of people to life, from street orators and ragamuffin rioters to impoverished duchesses. She told those readers who were expecting more description of scenes than of people: "I am more earnestly bent . . . upon availing myself of all my opportunities for listening to the conversation within the houses, than on contemplating all the marvels that may be seen without" (6). Sometimes she made herself a participant in debates, many of which provided an opportunity to air her own strong views.

In many of these dialogues her long-standing concern with the theme of women returned. What was woman's role in France? She records a lengthy discourse with a Frenchman on the fate of the great number of single women in England. He claims the redundancy of single females is no problem in France. Other letters record conversations discussing the variations between young married women's lives in England and in France, on young ladies and old ladies, on chaperones and flirtations. In England, young unmarried ladies are the center of society; in France wives are more important. Indeed, she noted, it is "as if the heart and soul of a French girl were asleep, or at least dozing, till the ceremony of marriage awakened them" (35).

In general, after observing the "character, position, and influence" of Parisian women, Trollope concludes that women play a distinguished part in French society and overall "have more power and more important influence than the women of England" (51). French politeness to women "is very far from superficial." They are shown real "domestic respect." Even more important, French ladies do not share that worst terror of young Englishwomen "of being called learned." In France no "*blue*" badge" is attached to female possessors of talent and information. Lecturing her own countrymen here, she recalls with sorrow how "the dread of imputed blueism weighs down many a bright spirit." In France, however, "the higher efforts of the female mind" are honored. Rebuked herself so many times by reviewers for treating subjects of serious import, and thus presumably beyond her ken, Trollope remarks of Parisian women that "even politics may be handled by them without danger."

Her political conservatism, as always, emerges clearly in the book. She opposes "any further trial of a republican form of government" as well as freedom of the press, "the most awful engine that Providence has permitted the hand of man to wield" (67). These strong opinions color her reporting of the Lyons trial, of the new literature of Balzac and George Sand, of the Exhibition of Living Artists at the Louvre. Still, her biases did not detract from the insights she had to offer. She could appreciate the gracefulness of Sand's style, even while disapproving of her morality. While she castigated Hugo's "corrupt creations," her descriptions projected their power. Her method and distinctive voice gave the book originality. But beyond her clever handling of materials lay the astute observations of an eye upon which little was lost. Her recording of the visible surface of French life and letters in 1835 make the book a rich resource of scenes, characters, and conversations which continue to bring the life of the period closer to the grasp of the social and intellectual historian.[25]

Vienna and the Austrians and *A Visit to Italy*

In April 1836 Trollope concluded an agreement with Bentley for two novels and two more travel books, one to be a "work describing Mrs. Trollope's Travels in Austria and more particularly her residence in Vienna, to be treated in a similar manner to her recent book called 'Paris and the Parisians,' " and "a similar account of her Travels and Residence in various parts of Italy."[26] It was an ambitious contract for a 57-year-old woman. That summer she left for Italy, by way of Vienna, with Tom and Cecilia. After a stop in Paris to see the Garnetts, they arrived in Vienna to begin the touring and socializing that was necessary to gather materials. By December, because her daughter's health had declined, she proposed a return to England before continuing to Italy. In her account to Bentley she cited professional reasons: "I would much rather that my book on Austria be published before my journey to Italy began. They must be quite distinct, and if possible, unconnected even in feeling."[27] Her publisher agreed, and by 4 July 1837, with her characteristically incredible energy, Trollope had her work on Austria ready for the press.

Although she brought to this book her usual talents for observations and dramatization, *Vienna and the Austrians* represented something of a decline. Her greatest gift had always been for sharp satiric caricature. But in Vienna she found only gorgeous scenery and a man who quickly became her hero, Prince Clemens von Metternich, Chancellor of Austria, whom she called "one of the most admirable characters that I have ever known." Flattered by his attentions and those of his family, Trollope settled into a dangerous content with all she saw.

Of course, she did not discard all the successful devices of her earlier works. In this book, too, she cast herself as the daring picaresque heroine. In one adventure she, Tom, and Hervieu outwit a landlord who wants more money and even threatens to kill them.

As a super-traveler, she again ascends mountains, visits the remotest waterfalls, and makes a dangerous descent to an underground salt mine. Pointedly, she reminds her readers about the difficulty of her voyages, about the "stout heart" needed to become "an *avant-couriere*" who describes things "as they are" (1:265). But in the second volume her inspiration flagged under the weight of her delight in Vienna's high society. Here she forgot dramatic anecdotes and lost herself in endless descriptions of festivities and names of the attending aristocracy. She detailed where she dined and wrote down a veritable litany of kings, queens, nobles, and other of the elite who crossed her path. Her place descriptions were conventional and uninteresting. She toured the principal churches and recorded her views of "noble landscapes." Frequently, she apologized for the tedium of such descriptions (1:155). From her journey out of Stuttgart, through the Tyrol to Vienna, to her residence and activities within Viennese society, the book lacked the sharp character of her previous works.

Her politics remained conservative. In a lengthy passage with which Metternich himself helped, she praised the Austrian system of government and outlined its intricacies. This bias enraged many English reviewers, in particular the critic of *The Athenaeum,* who wrote:

Mrs. Trollope is just the person to trumpet forth the virtues of a self-styled paternal government, to illustrate the animal satisfactions and material comforts of the pampered tradesmen of an aristocratic capital, and to mistake these for national prosperity; to rejoice in the gorgeous pageantry of doting feudality, and to calumniate (as far as such a writer's censure can prevail) whatever tends to enlarge the mind of man and to enoble his nature.[28]

The writer concluded: "She is more bigoted, more slavish, more intolerant, more common-place and unintellectual than usual; and of all her publications, this is the one we have read with most disgust and with less pleasure." But in addition to her usual penchant for offending liberal critics, Trollope had with her Vienna volumes also succeeded in creating a dull book!

A Visit to Italy completed her decline as a travel writer. Her major creative energy was now being poured into fiction, the most recent of which was reformist and satiric in nature, with caustic shrewd observations of people and manners. This approach had once accounted for her successes in the travel genre, and her first book had been an attack upon a country and a culture with which she had found herself seriously incompatible. For her last travel book, however, she chose a subject much written upon, and it became a panegyric rhapsody on a country and a culture she had long loved. The problem with *A Visit to Italy,* was not, however, solely one of manner and familiar material. In this book people recede to the background in favor of art, architecture, and the literature of the past. She who had been a pioneer in writing travel books that emphasized people rather than landscapes now shifted her focus:

Many other little details might be added, such as the daily assembling of market-carts, and the very unceremonious spreading out of sacks of grain and various other commodities upon the pavement . . . but all this is absolutely forgotten, overwhelmed and lost sight of, beside the vastness and dignity of the edifices (1:132–33).

Throughout the book, she preferred to describe the antiquities of Italy, its heritage of culture and art, and not its present appearance. After an annoyingly superficial description of Naples ("The people eat great quantities of maccaroni . . . make coral trinkets and cheap gloves" and have a theater which "is the largest in the world," (2:217–218), she confessed her own surprise at her concentration on antiquity: "I would not beforehand have believed it possible that I could have ever learned to care so much more about things that are not, than about things that are." But such was the prevailing pattern of her book.

In one passage she candidly noted: "I know I shall be involved in a sort of labyrinth of astonishment and admiration, which will make it exceedingly difficult to be intelligible" (2:75). And she repeatedly apologized to her readers: "I am almost afraid to ask you to go with me to the Pitti again lest you should fancy that I intend to turn myself into a catalogue, and then insist upon your reading me. But I will do no such thing" (1:155–156). Despite such resolutions, however, Trollope expatiated frequently upon her favorite artists—Veronese, Giotto, Donatello, Raphael, Verrocchio, Michelangelo, Andrea del Sarto, Rubens, Murillo, and Titian. She weakly concluded: "And now if I can help it, I will talk to you no more about the pictures of the Pitti Palace." But there followed page after page of descriptions of architectural monuments!

The book predictably contained comprehensive descriptions of Rome and St. Peter's during a papal mass, of Venice and Byron's Armenian convent, and even of recently discovered Pompeii. She made the requisite stop at Petrarch's house, where she picked a "passion flower" to serve as a relic of the visit. But while some scenes are competently drawn, the reader is inundated by an endless succession of churches, processions, palaces, the leaning tower, Brunelleschi's dome, and countless royal villas. Uncritical awe suffused her accounts. She approached Florence in a "fever of anticipation. . . . I almost felt as if I were going to enter bodily into the presence of Dante, Petrarch, and Boccaccio." And she asks after visiting the library of St. Lawrence: "Who can see the oldest manuscript of Virgil extant, and not feel that exciting species of curiosity, which is a sort of glory to feel and to indulge?" (1:183). At the end, Trollope herself was aware of the book's shortcomings: "Why should I recite the names of endless palaces and of temples sufficient to turn my pages into a Pantheon?" (2:355). But a pantheon it was, enshrining her love of Italy's past, providing no insights into the life of its people. The book was, on the whole, a failure. As one reviewer complained, "the last thing one should have expected from Mrs. Trollope is a work whose pages are characterless."[29]

Some have said that the traveler is always a person in search of himself. He travels, testing against a wide and changing reality that essential inner self about which he is still uncertain. If such had been, at least in part, Trollope's motives for her peripatetic life, in Italy the self and the environment became quickly one and, like most such loving encounters with what seemed to her perfection, left her characteristic voice silenced in uncritical awe. For Frances Trollope, a visit to Italy was an introduction to a permanent home and the end of her traveling and travel accounts.

Chapter Three
Fiction of Social Reform

Trollope's social reform fiction was a natural outgrowth of her travel books; it was just a short step from setting a mirror to the real world to trying to change the institutional deformities the mirror reflected. When she addressed herself more seriously to the fiction she was producing between journeys, she began to create truly original novels. She was certainly an early leader among those who were turning away from what George Eliot later called "silly novels" of romance and Gothic horror, to serious subjects of reform.[1] As a result of her interest in travel books, she had become an experienced observer of the social scene. In using novels to inform the public about the abuses that were part of the condition of the England in which they lived, Frances Trollope was the first to discover a remarkable number of fictional areas soon to be explored by other writers: negro slavery, hypocritical religious enthusiasm, child labor in the new industrialized cities, and the so-called "fallen-woman" issue.

Her contemporaries were shocked by the harsh bitterness of these novels, and for her pioneering efforts Frances Trollope was much maligned by critics and reviewers. Sixteen years after she presented her first reform novel to the public, the *Gentleman's Magazine*, in discussing the works of "The Lady Novelists of Great Britain," noted pointedly that although women had proven their talents at some kinds of novel-writing, "men have come to look with distrust on woman's championship of social questions" in reform fiction, where "they do often, certainly, go beyond the mark."[2] Unable to dispute her facts, critics directed their venomous attacks to her personality and sex and greeted her unusual subject matter by labeling these novels low, coarse, and vulgar, and her characters hideous, revolting, and repulsive. Even so perceptive a social observer as Thackeray agreed that Frances Trollope had embarked upon an unfortunate new fictional direction. His remarks are only one expression of the many such criticisms she received: "When suddenly, out of the gilt pages of a pretty picture book, a comic moralist rushes forward, and takes occasion to tell us that society is diseased, the laws unjust, the rich ruthless, the poor martyrs, the world lopsided, and *vice-versa*, persons who wish to lead an easy life are inclined to remonstrate against this literary ambuscade."[3] But Trollope ignored such lectures and was not to be deterred from the task of probing issues she thought her readers needed to consider.

Ironically, modern critics, now accustomed to fiction with a purpose, have downplayed her courage in thus selecting controversial subject matter and have questioned the sincerity of her interest in reform, calling her a woman "driven to writing because of financial distress" and thus anxious to give the public "what they want." The reviews of her reform fiction refute that allegation and present Trollope's achievement in a different light: it was not an easy or popular task that she assumed as she helped to shape a new sensibility toward the realistic social novel.[4]

Slavery: *The Life and Adventures of Jonathan Jefferson Whitlaw* (1836)

Trollope's first novel of social criticism was dedicated to "those states of the American Union in which slavery has been abolished, or never permitted." Her interest in the subject of slavery continued even after she had left Nashoba. From the first she had realized the dramatic potential of slavery. In *Domestic Manners* most of her treatments of this subject were cast along anecdotal, narrative lines, brief but telling vignettes. Now, four years later, and with three published novels to her credit, she became the first novelist to treat the evils of slavery for a wide reading public. The plot of *Jonathan Jefferson Whitlaw* made clear the most prominent abuses of the slavery system: the separation of families, the sexual exploitation of female slaves, the brutalizing of the owners themselves, the violence of the lynch law which made those who tried to resist fear for their lives. Frances Trollope explored these subjects with more frank realism than Harriet Beecher Stowe in her more famous antislavery novel, *Uncle Tom's Cabin* (1851), which appeared fully fifteen years after *Jonathan Jefferson Whitlaw* had made its more difficult way.

The story revolves completely around the subject of slavery. Jonathan Jefferson Whitlaw is born to a Mississippi squatter family that gets ahead through "calculation." Whitlaw senior, his wife, sister, and young son soon move up to better land and settle near

a family of German immigrants, the Steinmarks, who have cultivated land in the forests of Louisiana, significantly without employing a single slave. The Whitlaws are appropriately scornful:
"Nobody that was anybody would ever think of getting along without a slave. It was plain that, with all their big clearing and grand
house, the Steinmarks were nothing but a set of beggarly hard-
working foreigners, that did not know what it was to live like
gentlemen and Americans" (1:110). The Whitlaws feel differently,
and immediately purchase two slaves and send young Jonathan off
to school at Natchez, where he "had need of all his discretion to
conceal the outward expression of the joy he felt at being within
reach of daily watching the knaveries, cruelties, debaucheries, and
drunkenness never absent where a slave population disgraces the
soil, and which, if report say true, may be found in as great fulness
of abomination at Natchez as at any point of earth afflicted with
this curse" (1:111). The antagonism between the Whitlaws and the
Steinmarks, particularly with regard to slavery, forms a focus of the
novel.

Up in Natchez, young Jonathan meets an old acquaintance, Colonel Dart, the largest slave owner in the area, and soon becomes
Dart's confidential clerk at Paradise Plantation, with its five hundred
"negurs" who "sweat into dollars uncountable" (1:120). Dart lives
in fear, both of the Negroes and missionaries like Edward Bligh
who seems sent "on earth for the alone purpose of plaguing honest
men" (1:120). Whitlaw agrees to take over at the Plantation. "What's
freedom for," he asks Dart, "if we can't do what we like with our
own born slaves? There's nothing so dispisable in my mind as a
man what's afraid to kick the life out of his own nigger if he sees
good" (1:123). Upon thus uttering "the sentiments of a free people,"
Whitlaw is hired. Before long, he adds to his overseeing tasks the
subjecting of Dart's female slaves to his sexual advances. His bru-
tality in this matter startled readers unaccustomed to these frank
suggestions of sadistic behavior. When one girl tries to run away,
he is delighted. "She's a neat little craft for a nigger; and she'd skip
handsome over them stumps younder." After the girl is caught, she
freely offers her back for a beating, begging only the favor of remaining clothed throughout the ordeal. All at once, Whitlaw turns
vicious: "Strip, black toad—strip, or you shall be soaked in oil and
then singed" (1:218ff.). The scene is laced throughout with sexual
overtones.

Other characters complete the plot. Two separated slaves, Phebe and Caesar, are aided by the Steinmarks and the missionary Edward Bligh and his sister Lucy. They conspire to unite the lovers, even while Bligh's more serious purpose is "to preach the doctrine of hope and salvation to the despairing slaves" (1:187). Another of the book's major characters is Juno, an aged slave who manipulates Dart and Whitlaw through appealing to their superstition and ignorance. Though Whitlaw regards her as a sorceress, Juno is a real woman whom race and sex have robbed of her many children and made her an emotional automaton. She was sold to a succession of owners, who had used her sexually. Toward her children, who were sold as soon as they could work, she could afford to indulge no feeling, and she bore them "more like a well-regulated machine than a human being" (2:6). While young and beautiful, she had borne the baby of an English settler who educated the girl as his own and took her back to England, where she passed for white, and later married an Englishman. Juno, now an aged crone, avenges herself for her tragic life by making fools of her present owners, pretending to have magical powers even as she permits herself the luxury of one last dream: to be "ancestress of a very beautiful and glorious race" through her free English granddaughter, who of course has no idea of her racial backgrounds (2:12).

In one of the book's most dramatic uses of coincidence, Mr. Croft, the father of Juno's granddaughter Selina, has come to America to sell all his slaveholding lands, and brings his daughter with him. Whitlaw, as Dart's agent, offers to buy the land, but after meeting Selina seeks to marry her and thus acquire Croft's property for nothing. Selina, however, refuses him. The scorned Whitlaw learns the history of her parentage and tries blackmail, demanding her father's property in return for his silence. Selina foils his plan by committing a flowery and theatrical suicide.

Thus maddened, Whitlaw concentrates his evil efforts on the Blighs, who are hiding runaway slaves. In an exciting scene Lucy Bligh meets some Choctaw Indians in the forest who at first seem savage. Finally, fearing Whitlaw more, she asks for their help, finding "something . . . in the general appearance of the *civilized* man which terrified her more than the painted and scarred features of the Indians" (3:132). The scene has dramatic effect and also reinforces Trollope's theme: in a slave society those who are civilized have no place. As the novel shows, the sensitive and feeling ones

do not always succeed; a lynch party dispatched by Whitlaw catches
and murders Edward Bligh, but his sister escapes.

For a while Whitlaw seems to be triumphant, for when Dart
dies, he leaves all of Paradise Plantation to his former agent. But
Juno lures Whitlaw to the forest, where a group of slaves assassinates
him. She conceals his body with symbolic appropriateness: "It was
my child he killed and it was my hands that hollowed out his grave"
(3:336). Later, Whitlaw's good Aunt Clio inherits the property,
while the Steinmarks return to Europe with Phebe and Caesar.
Through the actions of a number of dedicated women, some of the
evils of slavery have been exposed and others mitigated.

In *Whitlaw* Trollope set the patterns that later writers of antislavery novels would eventually repeat. Overseers are sadistic. Slaves
are good, loving, and loyal. The American political system is helpless before the institution of slavery; the virtuous must escape to
other lands. Slave mothers lose their children, but they survive and
endure, to outlive their ignorant, tyrannical masters. While *Uncle
Tom's Cabin* is the best-known book of its kind, in conception and
execution it owes much to Trollope's prototype. Yet *Whitlaw* has
its own merits and is Trollope's first novel to show its creator's firm
and confident grasp of character, plot, and setting in the service of
an all-encompassing theme;' slavery is the rotten canker at the heart
of American life.

To advance this theme, Trollope made use of a number of settings,
from the isolated Mississippi backwoods, where the Whitlaws bru-
talize their household slaves, to the fiendishly efficient Paradise
Plantation, where Colonel Dart and Whitlaw work five hundred
slaves. Nearby, lies the productive, utopian farm Reichland, whose
European family is opposed to slaveholding. To these rural scenes
she adds the urban settings of Natchez and New Orleans, with their
outdoor slave sales, low shops, and quadroon balls. Inside the homes
of the southern slaveholding gentlemen, their childlike wives lux-
uriate and are cruel in their own petty ways, immobilized and
degraded on their pedestals from which they can do little beyond
tyrannizing the weak.[5]

Trollope's cast of character clearly brings the book's activist message across. Among the whites the man who tries to help the slaves
by preaching the nonviolent message of Christianity is lynched by
a degenerate mob. The "good" Europeans must flee America and
return to their native land. Only those who fight back are successful.

Her slave heroine, no pacifist or reconciled Uncle Tom, must finally resort to murdering Whitlaw, a deed which Frances Trollope leaves unpunished. Thus, the novel ends with decisive action, violent and illegal. Disenchanted herself by gradual, philanthropic efforts at coping with slavery, Trollope let her readers draw their own conclusions about possible remedies. The reaction of the literary journals showed that she had found her mark. *The Athenaeum* called *Whitlaw* an unpleasant and repulsive book; *The Spectator* criticized her unfavorable portrayal of southern planters who were, it insisted, "the gentlemen of the States." Fifty years later her sympathetic daughter-in-law thought the tale was "painful" and questioned the appropriateness of using such unhappy subject matter as the basis of fiction. In general, Trollope was accused of extravagance and misrepresentation. Yet today *Whitlaw* is a novel that demands respect for its serious treatment of an important subject. Slave narratives have since documented the book's powerful scenes of torture and degradation, and historians have generally confirmed the truth of what she wrote about the social disintegration in a slaveholding population. Her blend of fact and fiction had succeeded in bringing a controversial subject to a wide audience. Within a year, the book went through three editions and launched Frances Trollope as a pioneer in writing fiction with a social purpose.[6]

The Abuses of Evangelicalism: *The Vicar of Wrexhill* (1837)

Trollope saw the controversy surrounding her slavery book as a sign that she was no mere writer of popular pap, but a woman who had the power to effect change in society. Thus, immediately upon completing *Whitlaw*, she turned her critical eye upon a subject nearer to home, then much debated, the abuses inherent in the more fervent versions of evangelicalism. In her *Vicar of Wrexhill* she continued to provoke the critics who found her persistent interest in dissecting painful subjects inappropriate for any author of popular novels, above all, for a woman. As one noted scathingly:

She scents out moral deformities with a sort of professional eagerness, and applies herself to their exposure, regardless of the uncleanness into which her task may lead. . . . In her last novel she plunged over head into the abominable sink of slavery; here again, she is up to her neck in another kennel of corruption—*The Vicar of Wrexhill* being a tale written for the express purpose of *showing up* the errors of a sect increasingly prevalent and powerful among us—the Evangelicals.[7]

Her plot clearly illustrated the baneful effects of religious fervor, particularly in the lives of women. A Mrs. Mowbray regains her large dowry upon the death of her husband, who thus has left in her hands the task of making separate arrangements for their three grown children. The new widow, weak and dependent, thus becomes the prey of Mr. Cartwright, the Vicar of Wrexhill, who plots to marry her for her money. Although his techniques of frequent private prayer sessions laced with heavy emotionalism alienate two of the three children, he nevertheless insinuates himself into Mrs. Mowbray's affections and marries her. A cruel and ungenerous stepfather to the son and elder daughter, he turns the full force of his passionate religiosity upon the youngest daughter, who, like her mother, is attracted by his black eyes and caressing hands. Eventually young Fanny sees his true character, but Mrs. Mowbray remains deluded. She bears the Vicar an heir, but then she and the child fall fatally ill. Only on her deathbed she discovers the Vicar's true nature and makes a will leaving everything to the rightful heirs. At last the arch-hypocrite retires from the scene, and rational religion and virtue triumph.[8]

This novel continues Trollope's particular interest in the unfortunate effects of evangelicalism upon women. As one of her characters says of "this insidious and most anti-Christian schism": "It has been the young girls who have been selected as the first objects of conversion and then made the active means of spreading it afterwards" (2:39-40). The Vicar rests "all his hopes of fame, wealth and station on the power he can obtain over women" (1:286). All his influence is over the female part of his congregation, with whom he prays, exhorts, sings, sets to work on fancy fairs, and encourages in the writing of tracts "to dispose of their superfluous time" (2:262). In other moments of privacy, under the lime tree in the garden, he kisses, cajoles, and caresses to get his way. Many reviewers attacked Trollope for having made the influence of evangelicals on women "the groundwork of her book" and found this "sort of leering jocularity unbefitting in her—disgusting, when considered with reference to the subject."[9]

Trollope's portrait of the Reverend Mr. Cartwright is a hostile one, a study in "clerical beastliness." The Vicar's talent is for honeyed eloquence, and he expresses himself "with an unusual flow of words, in sentences particularly well-constructed," yet keeps his opinions "enveloped in a mist" (1:127). The oily and lascivious Vicar exchanges kisses "of holy peace and brotherly love" with the more attractive young ladies (3:60), yet to others he is mean and malicious, chuckling in delight ("It was the hosannah of a fiend," 3:73), over the troubles of a ruined curate whose wife is ill with brain fever and whose children are starving. Trollope gave her vicar all those vices associated with the worst types of evangelical parson—sloth, malice, rapacity, a smooth tongue, ignorance of true religion, overarching hypocrisy, and a prurient flirtatiousness. The reviewers protested not only the harsh portrayal of the Vicar ("He glides on his way like a serpent—glossy, silent, and poisonous"), but the appropriateness of a woman's selecting such a subject for a novel. "His is a fearful character; and some of his later doings are too dark and terrible to have been written down by a woman."[10]

The many unfavorable critical attacks on *The Vicar of Wrexhill* served only to enhance the novel's favorable reception with the public, who found it topical in subject matter and, particularly in its strong portrayal of the Vicar, original in characterization. And throughout even the most critical reviews ran an undercurrent of praise for the forceful conception. *The Examiner's* appraisal was typical and revealed the difficulty reviewers faced in handling this unusual fictional material: "The character is revolting; many of the scenes described are eminently disgusting and repulsive, but there is extraordinary power about them nevertheless."[11] This novel's success, together with the increasing expenses of her travels, surely confirmed Trollope in her decision to pursue further the writing of realistic social fiction. Her next work would address an even more hotly contended and inflammatory subject.

Child Labor in the Factories: *The Life and Adventures of Michael Armstrong, the Factory Boy* (1840)

Two years after completing *The Vicar of Wrexhill* Trollope decided to write a novel exposing the horrors of factory conditions in England. It was again a topical subject. Since 1831 advocates of reform had mounted a widespread campaign to limit the number of hours that children and women could work in factories. The revelations of the Sadleir Committee had shocked England, as had the numerous pamphlets and broadsides, especially those published under the agency of *The Northern Star*, a Chartist-oriented newspaper of the industrial Midlands. Frances Trollope had followed this printed campaign with both interest and concern. In the winter of 1839 she decided to go and see for herself the situation in Manchester and, with letters of introduction from Lord Shaftesbury, arranged to meet many of the most prominent agitators for reform—Richard Oastler, the "king of Lanceshire"; Joseph Raynor Stephens, a fiery and dynamic preacher; and a Mr. J. Doherty, a bookseller who had printed a pamphlet exposing the evils of the apprenticeship system. She made no secret of the underlying purpose of her trip. *The Northern Star* editorialized: "We have heard that it is her intention to lend the whole power of her vigorous pen to the great object of THE EMANCIPATION OF OUR WHITE NEGROES. The lash of her satire has already been felt by the slave owners on the other side of the Atlantic."[12]

Bringing to bear the full experience of her career as an observant traveler, Trollope, in a short three weeks, managed to visit some typical factories, meet the main reform leaders, and visit the slum homes of the workers. She also procured a copy of the Doherty pamphlet, the memoirs of one Robert Blincoe, a valuable eyewitness account. Together with her own observations and conversations with the knowledgeable men of the day, the Blincoe memoir gave her the focus for her novel and a model for her young hero. She used the Blincoe pamphlet ("A Memoir of Robert Blincoe, an Orphan Boy: Sent from the Workhouse of St. Pancras, London, at Seven Years of Age, to endure the Horrors of a Cotton-Mill, through his infancy and Youth, with a Minute Detail of his Sufferings, being the First Memoir of the Kind Published" 1832) for details of food and diet, living conditions, characters of overseers and children, and dramatic anecdotes.[13] Thus, the Blincoe memoir became a source book, in somewhat the same manner as her American travel account had for *Jonathan Jefferson Whitlaw*.

The authenticity of *Michael Armstrong* grew out of her methods of research and composition. It is a measure of her talents as an observer that she was able to glean as much material as she did from her relatively short visit. Aware that some of her scenes might seem incredible (like the one in which the apprentice boys must struggle with the hogs for their food), Trollope insisted upon her accuracy within the story itself: "Let none dare to say this picture is exaggerated, till he has taken the trouble to ascertain by his own personal investigation that it is so" (186).[14] And while many did protest, especially the advocates of laissez faire, contemporary documents bear out the truth of her descriptions. As an accurate portrayal of Manchester Life, her book would not be equalled until later in the century when Elizabeth Gaskell, herself a Manchester resident, composed *Mary Barton* (1848) and *Ruth* (1853).

Because she was so convinced herself of the truth of her story, Trollope sought a method of publication that would bring her novel to the widest possible readership. Determined to reach "many thousands of her countrymen," she chose to write *Michael Armstrong* in shilling monthly numbers. This method presented several problems. Because of the mass audience, the literary establishment regarded the method as slightly disreputable, especially for a woman author. But she went ahead because her purpose was serious. As one reviewer noted of *Michael Armstrong*: "It seeks at once to impress a deep moral lesson and to work a great social change."[15] Also, despite Dickens's successes with monthly numbers, many literary critics attacked the aesthetic weaknesses of serial publication as leading to sprawling plots and unfocused narratives, lasting, as it customarily did, over a period of a year and a half. And indeed, *Michael Armstrong* does suffer from some flaws of plotting attributable to its method of composition and publication. Trollope fails to fuse the two main plot strands, the story of Michael Armstrong's sufferings, which dominate the early part of the book, and Mary Brotherton's awakening to the realities of the industrial system, the main emphasis in the second half. But as a whole, the book is unified by its consistent theme (for both Michael and Mary, public legislation is the answer to the problems produced by the new factories) and its powerful Manchester settings. It retains an interest for the modern reader as an important achievement in the use of fiction for political and social agitation.

Theme and setting also gave the novel its innovativeness. *Michael Armstrong* was an early criticism of the effectiveness of private philanthropy and presented powerful arguments that only public legislation (in particular the Ten Hours Bill) could bring relief to the sufferings of the industrial poor. The novel was also the first to set

a significant amount of plot action directly in the grim urban en-
virons, rendering in sharp detail the living conditions of an industrial
hell and describing factory conditions and child labor among the
machines for middle-class readers unfamiliar with the settings or
terminology of industrialization. Trollope's story which set forth in
fearful scenes the "earracking sounds," the nauseous air, the "hundreds
of helpless children," and the "monstrous chamber," was a vivid
exposure of the sights, sounds, and smells of "the factory system
in all its branches" (80-83), the first comprehensive treatment of
the industrial wasteland in English fiction.

The book was also unique in its avoidance of pious Christian
rationalizaton about the sufferings of the poor, in the style of Trollope's contemporary Mrs. Tonna.[16] Trollope is interested in this
earth, not in the kingdom of heaven. When a little factory girl
claims to be glad about a friend's death ("She will not be hungry
in Heaven . . . nor will she work till she is ready to fall and surely
God will give us green fields and sweet fresh air in Heaven"), Michael
Armstrong cries out in protest: "I wouldn't be glad if you was to
die" (212-13). Trollope's book arises from a different attitude, no
less Christian than Mrs. Tonna's, that the lives of the workers must
be made decent upon this earth.

As the story opens, young Michael Armstrong, a factory boy of
seven, is befriended by Sir Matthew Dowling, a rich manufacturer
who uses this so-called benevolence to defuse the anger surrounding
the accidental death of a young girl in one of his factories. His
overseer concurs with the ruse, complaining of "all the grunting
and grumbling we hear about overworked children." The doctor in
charge of the factory children also agrees that "the nimbleness of
children" is absolutely necessary in factories: "Upon my soul," he
advises Sir Matthew, "if I were you, I would build a meeting house
. . . and hire a preacher" to preach against those protesting the
factory conditions (77-78). Thus Trollope makes clear from the very
start of her story the conspiracy of silence that operated against the
factory children among those in power.

Soon Sir Matthew tires of his benevolence toward the dirty little
piecer, and sends Michael away as an apprentice to Deep Valley
Mills, a horrible establishment which exploits the labor of unwanted
and orphaned children. The second line of the plot begins when a
rich heiress, Mary Brotherton, interests herself in Michael and goes
in search of him. She is, in part, a persona for Trollope herself, as

she interviews Michael's family and other laborers in their slum dwellings, doggedly pursuing her intention to learn more about the system.[17] The plot moves along here by means of a series of interrogative dialogues, sparse question-and-answer sessions, which give an aura of reality, resembling as they do the published Parliamentary Commission reports, with the relentless, dispassionate questions, and the matter-of-fact yet pathetic answers of those being examined. In the novel Mary's interviews of the Drake family bring the life of slum and factory solidly into the story line. Mary asks why the oldest child is home tending his mother and the younger ones are at the factory.

> "They won't have me now, 'cause of this" . . . the child held up a little shrivelled right hand, three fingers of which had a joint deficient. "I can't piece now, and so they won't let me come."
>
> "And Sophy won't let me go, 'cause of this," said the little one . . . displaying the limb swollen and discoloured, from some violent contusion.
>
> " . . . how did you do this? . . . "
>
> "Twas the billy-roller. . . ."
>
> "But how did it happen, my child? Did some part of the machinery go over you?"
>
> "No! That was me," cried the elder . . . holding up his demolished fingers. "Twas the stretcher's billy-roller as smashed Becky."

Miss Brotherton is incredulous. "But these bruises could not be the effect of a beating." Yet the mother replies, "Why, ma'am, the billy-roller as they beats 'em with is a stick big enough to kill with; and many and many is the baby that has been crippled with it" (127-28).

A second interview reveals the living conditions of the factory children at home:

> "You seem all of you greatly in want of clothes. How comes that, when so many of the family work, and get wages?"
>
> "The wages isn't enough to buy us bread, ma'am," replied the eldest girl, "and help pay lodging rent. . . ."
>
> "I suppose when you say bread, you mean food of all kinds?—and tea, and sugar, and butter, and so on?" said Mary.

"I have not had the taste of meat in my mouth for above these two years . . . and as to sugar in our tea, or butter on our bread, no factory child is brought up to it. . . ."

"Do not be angry with me, Sophy," said she, "if I ask questions that seem unfeeling and very ignorant. I really know little or nothing about the manner in which poor people live, and I want to know. Not merely from curiosity, but because I should like to help them if I could."

More questions follow, about their father, his drinking, the exhaustion of the children: "Do you mean, that the children work til they are so tired as to fall asleep standing?" Miss Brotherton learns the children begin work at age five and don't learn to read or sew. So-called "Sunday schools" are of no avail because "when the Sunday comed we couldn't sit down upon the bench, neither Grace, nor Dick, nor I, without falling dead asleep." This interview ends with a graphic description of the end of the day for one factory child:

"I have seen poor mother . . . lay little Becky here, down upon the bundle of straw that she and I sleeps upon, 'cause she couldn't keep her up to eat her supper when she comed from the mill—and I have seen her put the sopped bread in her mouth when she was so dead asleep, that she couldn't get her to swallow it—and how could she or the rest of us learn to read, ma'am?" (153-55).

The third interview, called in its chapter title "A Voyage of Discovery," is between Mary Brotherton and the enlightened reformer, Reverend George Bell of Fairley (modeled on Parson Bull of Brierly, known widely as the "Ten-Hours Parson."). [18] With him, Mary moves beyond the specifics of the factory childrens' plight to a realization of the broader economic realities and a discussion of possible solutions. Mary's questions of Bell lead him into some of the most important theoretical ideas of the novel. "Alas! Alas! cries Mary, "Is it thus my wealth has been accumulated? . . . Is there no power in England, sir, righteous and strong enough to stay this plague?" (202). Calling the factory system "destructive of every touch of human feeling," Bell explains how "the low-priced agony of labouring infants is made to eke out and supply all that is wanting to enable the giant engines of our factories to outspin all the world!" He explains the hopeless life-cycle of the poor, the mechanical drudgery, the early, thoughtless marriages, and the large families produced to meet the ceaseless need for cheap, unskilled labor. "By degrees, both the husband and the wife find employment in the factory less certain. It is for children, children, children, that the unwearied engines call." Bell draws a dramatic picture of the subsequent degradation of family life and "the dark little circle in which they move from birth to death" (203-4).[19] Mary's next questions lead to Trollope's main theme: "In what way . . . is it wished, or hoped, that the legislature should step forward to cure this dreadful evil?" Bell's answer provides the book's solution: "All that the poor creatures ask for themselves, is that by act of Parliament it should be rendered illegal for men women and children to be kept to the wearying unhealthy labour of the mills for more than 10 hours out of every day, leaving their daily wages at the same rate as now" (206).

Miss Brotherton's questions continue and leave her convinced that "the hope I had nourished of making my fortune useful to the suffering creatures among whom I live, is vain and idle." Individual benevolence—"organizing schools, founding benefit societies,"—all such sporadic charities are useless "to beings so crushed, so toil-worn, and so degraded" (208-9). Through this dialogue-question technique, often employed by the author in her travel books and fully harmonious with her theme and material, Trollope underlines her point: all England lives in ignorance, and it is only by questioning that the truth can be learned and any progress can be made. Englishmen living comfortably must ponder Mary Brotherton's anguished cry: "I too am living by the profit of the factory house. Is this division just?—oh, God! Is it holy?" (137).

The didactic aspects of this section are dominant and the plot somewhat contrived. Hearing that Michael Armstrong has died at Deep Valley, Mary Brotherton abandons her search, but not before she has rescued from the factory Michael's friend Fanny Fletcher and his brother Edward. That much, at least, an individual can do. In the third volume the reader learns that Michael is alive and has escaped from Deep Valley. At eighteen, he is returning to his family at Ashleigh after years as an agricultural laborer, when he finds a heap of handbills calling a general meeting to sign a petition limiting the hours of factory labor to ten:

Michael Armstrong was no longer a factory operative; free as the air he breathed upon his beloved mountaintops, he no longer trembled at the omnipotent frown of an overlooker, nor sickened as he watched the rising

sun that was to set again long hours before his stifling labours ceased. . . .
Yet did his heart throb, and his eye kindle as he perused page after page
of the arousing call which summoned tens of thousands, nay hundreds of
thousands to use the right their country vested in them, of imploring
mercy and justice from the august tripartite power that ruled the land.
(312)

As Michael reads the simple eloquence of these appeals, he is
filled with emotion: "Such terribly true representations were found
among them of the well-remembered agonies of his boyhood. that
Michael was fain to put his spread hand before his face to conceal
the emotions they produced." He determines "to attend . . . and
hold up his hand for the ten hours bill" (312-13), giving the novel
its most crucial plot action. More important than Michael's successful escape and subsequent fortunate marriage is the "wonderful
and spirit-stirring spectacle" of this great assembly of human beings,
thousands moving together, joined under "the triumphant influence
of reason and kindness."

The very sight of the road along which he traveled, which looked like a
dark and mighty current moving irresistibly along, while tributary streams
flowed into it on all sides, so thick and serried was the mass that moved
along it, was of itself well worth the toil it cost him, to behold its peaceful
tumult. (314)

It was in the force of that great "current," both peaceful and tu-
multuous, that Trollope placed her hopes in this novel.
    At the end of the book a now bankrupt Sir Matthew falls ill, and
in a lengthy, melodramatic vision (drawn in a Goyaesque print by
Hervieu) all the "dirty, beastly factory-children" surround him.
"Their arms and legs are all broken and smashed, and hanging by
bits of skin. Take them away" (364), shouts a delirious Sir Matthew.
Meanwhile, Michael Armstrong, conveniently present, prays to
Heaven "that he might never be placed in any circumstances likely
to harden his heart, and make him the cause of suffering to others,—
a fearful and a dreadful crime" (366). Afterwards, Michael is reunited with his brother Edward, Mary Brotherton, and Fanny
Fletcher, whom he thought dead. Before long Mary and Edward,
Fanny and Michael confess mutual love and retire, "two very loving
and happy pairs" to a Rhinegau paradise which contains a separate
home for the couples, "each having its suite of drawing-rooms,

boudoirs, nurseries, school-rooms, *etcetera"* (386). This romantic, tagged-on ending contrasts sharply with the vivid realism of the rest of the novel.

In *Michael Armstrong* Trollope's main artistic success is in her careful renderings of three important industrial settings: the Ashleigh slum, Brookford factory, and the Mill at Deep Valley. Here again her sense of the importance of place is evident. These vividly described settings were an important means of conveying social information to her readers. Ashleigh was a "long, closely-packed double row of miserable dwellings, crowded to excess by the population drawn together by the neighboring factories" (35). Although lacking some of the metaphoric power of Dickens's vision of Coketown in *Hard Times* (1854), her descriptions of the urban slums had their own poetic force, in which the key element is always smoke and steam. Here were "forests of tall bare chimneys, belching eternal clouds of smoke" which "rear their unsightly shafts towards the sky" (144-45). The factories themselves were filled with "the whirling hissing world of machinery," with its "hot and tainted atmosphere," and "stench and stunning terrifying tumult" (237). Here, no one can speak without shouting. The third setting, Deep Valley, Trollope had not personally seen, but used the Blincoe pamphlet to depict the remote area where parish pauper children were sent to work in the mills. Repeatedly, she insists upon the accuracy of these descriptions, adding a pointed footnote about her sources and labeling the chapter "a faithful description of a valley in Derbyshire."

Supporting the author's verbal descriptions and settings were Hervieu's superb set of plates. They too tell the powerful story. "Michael Armstrong's Introduction to Dowling Lodge" shows a ragged Michael surrounded by the servant staff, who obviously consider themselves above him. The lordly butler, scorn upon his face, "my lady's own maid," holding a scent bottle to her nose to ward off the smell of the factory boy, an extremely fat and business-like cook—Hervieu's picture shows clearly that Michael can expect no sympathy from the household help. In other pictures Sir Matthew's superintendents appear as overweight or almost moronic, gross, and insensitive types, thick-lipped, vacant-eyed, in contrast to the thin, downcast little Michael. Another plate illustrates the slums, another the death of a poor woman on her straw bed, surrounded by her grieving family. In general the plates illustrate the book's most pathetic scenes: apprentices vying with hogs for food, a sad but determined mother lifting her sinking child from the snow, helping her onward toward the smoking factory which looms in the rear, while huddled shapes wait in the cold for the locked doors to open. Still another shows a ragged, angry father, carrying a "young victim of unnatural labor."

One of the plates, ironically entitled "Love conquered Fear," has, in its power and simplicity, become the standard illustration of the evils of child labor in the factory.[20] Hervieu renders the ragged, grimy-faced factory children at work, a haggard girl overseeing the looms, a small child crawling underneath to pick up scraps. In the background the well-clothed overseers, carrying clubs, converse with one another. In the center a delicate, cleaned-up Michael tearfully embraces his lame brother. All around, the regular looms and barred windows provide an inhuman backdrop to the boy's emotions.

One final illustration deserves notice: Hervieu's depiction of Michael Armstrong's subsequent contemplation of suicide. On a rocky precipice Michael stands across from "a multitude of cotton-factories, with their tall chimneys mocking the heavens" (300). The emaciated young man seems feverish and crosses his arms across his sunken chest, looking upwards, but the heavens show forth nothing but smoke. To his right, one withered, but obviously dying tree is all that interrupts the starkness of the plate, which contrasts pointedly with the plush bourgeois interiors of other illustrations. From his unconventional caricatures of American life in *Domestic Manners* and his brooding scenes of slavery in *Whitlaw*, to his depictions of the oily Vicar of Wrexhill, Hervieu had been an invaluable collaborator with Frances Trollope. In *Michael Armstrong* his drawings match the bitterness of the text.

Successful as her settings were, characterization was a problematic area. Trollope's characters are not complex and do not develop significantly. They were drawn primarily to illustrate and emphasize her social thesis, yet they have life and interest enough to carry the reader through the plot.[21] Sir Matthew Dowling is a completely evil and sadistic villian with no redeeming qualities. Michael Armstrong is the opposite of Dowling and his cronies, kind and good throughout, despite the abuses to which he is subjected. As his friends agree at the book's conclusion, "Michael Armstrong is a hero; he is our hero" (377). For the Victorian reader, his trials in factory and mill made Trollope's social message even more poignant. She knew, as did Dickens, the emotional capital to be made out the sufferings of the young. She drew a more convincing portrait of one of the reformers she herself had met, Parson Bull of Brierly (Bell, in the book). His position on factory legislation is clearly presented, even if not completely integrated with the story. But, through his fictional character, she brought the real man's reasonable, if impassioned arguments for legislative intervention to a wider audience than he could ever have gained from the pulpit.

As was increasingly becoming the case, Trollope was best in delineating female characters. Mary Brotherton, the wealthy heroine, is a forceful, independent woman, who arranges her own life. Like her creator, she determines to seek out the causes of these terrible conditions. Despite the horror of her friends and relatives, she resolves to help and even visits the factory districts to gain firsthand knowledge. Sir Matthew is distressed: "Gracious Heaven! You are not going to speak to those creatures. . . . I give you my sacred honour that I think you are very likely to be robbed and murdered if you approach the thresholds of such dwellings as those" (126). Mary Brotherton's reply is characteristic: "You must excuse me if I obstinately persevere in judging for myself," and sounds a new voice for women. She is a precursor of Trollope's many defiant heroines yet to come.

The explosive effect of *Michael Armstrong* was not lost upon Trollope's contemporaries, some of whom saw her as one more type of the so-called "physical force orators." And while men like Richard Oastler had been imprisoned for his seditious talk, *The Athenaeum's* reviewer thought "the author of *Michael Armstrong* deserves as richly to have eighteen months in Chester Goal as any that are there now for using violent language against the 'monster cotton mills.' " Supporting those whom Trollope had dubbed the "millocrats," the critic concluded: "Mill owners cannot refuse the smallest economy that offers in working the mills, on pain of ruin; and without forfeiting a claim to common humanity, they may be brought to look on the sufferings of their operatives, as a general looks on the carnage and mutilation of his soldiers."[22]

But Trollope would not accept the sufferings of children as the price for the economic welfare of the country. She wrote to expose "that hideous mystery by which the delicate forms of young children . . . mix and mingle with the machinery, from whence flows the manufacturers' wealth" (79). Her visit to Manchester, her talks with political radicals and the laborers of the factories had made her a

literary agitator in the cause of factory legislation. Like her character
Mary Brotherton, she had made a "voyage of discovery" and she
would never forget the lessons it had taught her. *Michael Armstrong*
proved a huge success, appearing in parts and then in both one-
volume and three-volume editions. The first printings rapidly sold
out, and it went into frequent reprints. After *Domestic Manners*, it
remains today her most famous and artistically satisfying book.

The Fallen Woman: *Jessie Phillips,*
A Tale of the Present Day (1843)

Undaunted by critical attacks, Trollope persisted in using controversial subject matter in her fiction. Three years after the appearance of *Michael Armstrong*, she became an advocate of reform of
the New Poor Law of 1834, the enactment of which had drastically
changed English traditions of relief for the poor. Laissez-faire econ-
omists and intellectuals alike had opposed the old welfare arrangements as unrealistic, and a dangerous interference with the free
market economy, because they destroyed people's incentive to work
and encouraged population growth among the poor. The New Poor
Law was designed to make welfare payments both difficult to get
and undesirable to receive because relief was only obtainable when
those in need entered union workhouses, which were deliberately
made as unpleasant as possible. This change from the Elizabethan
provisions, which had given relief in the home, contained a new
assumption, indicative of an altered consciousness, namely, that
poverty was caused by idleness or vice and should accordingly be
punished by imprisonment and disgrace.

Trollope's novel attacked the logic of the new law and exposed
the inhuman conditions in the workhouses. Her opposition to these
changes rose out of her conservatism and basic Christian principles
and was consistent with her previous concern for humanity's outcasts:
Negro slaves, the poor, and factory children. In *Jessie Phillips* she
turned her novelistic eye upon the poor again, this time in particular
upon their most desperate member, the fallen woman. The fate of
Jessie Phillips hinges on the changes in the law, especially its an-
cillary bastardy clauses, under which men were, for the first time
in England, sheltered from lawsuits in paternity cases.[23] Jessie's
story, and that of several minor characters, illustrate the inherent
evils of the new welfare system.

The novel is set in rural Deepbrook, amid a country gentry society whose most prominent family is the Daltons, with ten daughters and one son. Mr. Dalton has just been named to the newly appointed Board of Guardians who, under a Mr. Mortimer, a commissioner from London, is to administer the New Poor Law. There are dinner parties in which the leading citizenry debate the merits and drawbacks of the now rigidly centralized welfare system, and several people speak against this "fearful change in the treatment of the poor" (16).[24] The squire's son, Frederic, however, is more interested in women than Poor Laws. Vicious and unprincipled, he is glad enough of the provisions in the new law prohibiting paternity suits, which leave him free to indulge his inclinations for Jessie Phillips, a seamstress, and "the most beautiful girl in the country" (33). Jessie believes Dalton will eventually marry her, but only after safely inheriting his father's property. As Frederic claims, "should I marry without his consent before I am thirty, I forfeit every acre of it" (70). Thus, with false promises, Dalton seduces the girl who, "blindfolded and infatuated by her own passionate fancies," loves him. When Jessie becomes pregnant, Dalton abandons her, and the parish ladies, scandalized by her obvious condition, give her no more work. Aware of his legal immunity, Dalton offers her no support money for his illegitimate child. After Jessie's mother dies and her confinement approaches, she is forced to enter the Union Workhouse. Thus Trollope fuses the two major focuses of her novel in Jessie's story.

Jessie is not the only character whose fate is used to illustrate the evils of the new law. The widow Greenhill, who gives her small annuity to pay her son's debts, and needs assistance, is told to come into the workhouse along with her daughter-in-law and six grandchildren. The widow appears before the Board of Guardians to request an exemption on the basis of her own exemplary character, and is rudely treated. "It's capital fun," one guardian remarks, "to see her stand there with her threadbare old things put on with as many pins, and as much nicety, as if she had been dressing for court, and she looking all the time so very considerable more than half starved" (77). All pleas in her behalf by those who know her well are turned down in the interest of rigid adherence to the letter of the new law. "What is the use of centralization, which is becoming our blessing and our boast, you know, and what's the use of it, if we administer the law according to our local knowledge of individuals instead of according to the act?" (81). One guardian concludes: "The relief is to come, sir, just like the sun and the rain, upon the good and upon the bad, all alike. No difference, no preference, no good character, no bad character, to make any change or alteration whatever" (82). While the widow awaits the result of her plea, she talks to workhouse inmates and learns about life inside. There is no useful work to do, "unless you choose to beat stinking hemp" (83). Instead, men, women, and children, separated into groups without regard for family ties, are "made to sit all of a row in this dismal little den of a hole" (84). An anonymous gift from Squire Dalton's daughter Ellen, however, rescues the widow who can return to her own home.

Jessie, however, must enter the workhouse, and she too is duly humiliated before being permitted entrance. She must wear "the strictly regulated dress of the Union," and cut off her "luxuriant chestnut tresses." She must associate with not only the poor, but prostitutes and vicious criminals. She is not even permitted to walk outside. All this information, Trollope hopes, "will not have been altogether thrown away; [if] the gentle reader, in his easy chair, shall be permitted to profit by her experience" (192). The plot now alternates between conversations about the new law by the guardians and others of the Deepbrook gentry, and depictions of Jessie's misery in the workhouse. The author felt the strain in fusing the dramatic and didactic parts of her story and confesses to her readers: "It is very difficult to touch on any of the most mischievous points of this ill-digested law without being led to dwell upon them till the thread of the story is dropped and almost forgotten; but this will be considered as excusable by all who take a real interest in the subject, and for the rest—their disapprobation must be patiently endured" (210).

One of the most original parts of Trollope's plot is the way in which the women take the initiative. Widow Greenhill jeopardizes her own freedom to aid her son and his family. Ellen Dalton, Frederic's quiet but determined oldest sister, risks disclosure of a secret love in helping the widow. Jessie herself has a strong enough personality to approach a lawyer to learn her rights after failing to win from Dalton "provision for her child" (246). The really strong woman, however, is Martha Maxwell. Undeceived by Dalton's subsequent proposal of marriage to her, she allies herself with the rejected Jessie to whom she promises help: "Jessie Phillips, it shall not be my fault if justice be not done you" (173). Despite the risk to her own reputation, she visits Jessie in the workhouse and sets about trying to force Frederic to help Jessie. Trollope pointedly notes for the reader: "Whether Miss Maxwell was consummately wise and perfectly right in making this visit, or rather in saying all the comforting words she did in the course of it, is another affair. It is extremely possible that many very sensible persons may think this doubtful" (173). Martha tries blackmail (using Dalton's written promise of marriage to herself) and legal means (visits to another lawyer) to secure Jessie some aid for her as-yet-unborn child. She even tries to lecture Frederic on his responsibilities. Taken together, the women of this novel are the most important agents of the plot.

The men are weak or vicious. The elder Dalton, despite his money and influence, does little. Mortimer, the Commissioner, is ineffective. He spends most of his time rejecting invitations to discuss the merits of the New Poor Law. For him, his job is to administer the law, not to think or examine its merits. The lawyers are equally uninterested in any questions of absolute right and wrong, but engage themselves only in legalities, such as who has the right to sue. As one tells Jessie: "If it turns out, indeed, that you can't manage to maintain [the child] yourself, and that it is actually and *bona fide* thrown upon the rate-payers, why then *they* may look about them, if they like it, and if they can prove, without any help of yours, mind you, that this one or that one is the father, why then, by bringing forward their proof, they may make him just pay the workhouse charges, and no more. But *you*, and the likes of you, have no more to do with it than the man in the moon" (383-84). Frederic, of course, is the book's absolute and heartless villain. When confronted by Martha Maxwell's arguments over his responsibilities to Jessie, he pointedly refers to the bastardy clauses of the new law. "As if it did not happen every day in the year? What's that blessed clause in the new law for, I wonder, if a man is to be frightened out of his wits by such a matter as this?" (243).

After Jessie is rejected by the courts and responsible officials, she collapses, bears her child, and falls into a coma. Through a series of mixups and machinations, Dalton finds the child and murders it. Nearly senseless, and ignorant of who could have killed her baby, Jessie is accused and taken to prison. There she comes to doubt her own innocence; Martha Maxwell, however, remains a firm supporter. A jury believes she did commit the murder, but finds her not guilty by reason of insanity. Jessie dies before learning of her acquittal. Her defenders, especially Martha and Ellen Dalton, however, are not satisfied by the verdict, and confront Frederic who, aware of his guilt and fearful of exposure as the murderer of his own child, throws himself into a raging stream and drowns, a melodramatic form of suicide more often associated with fallen women in the Victorian novel than with their seducers.

The vivid episodes of Trollope's novel had great effect on public opinion, more than Oastler's pamphlets ("The Right of the Poor to Liberty and Life," Liverpool, 1838) or the Rev. Stephens's dramatic sermons ("The spirit of all our laws is a spirit breathing hatred to the poor.").[25] *Jessie Phillips* brought home to the middle-class reader, as no one had before, the callous insensitivity that permeated the official attempts to aid the "other England." The literary critics quickly noted the connections between this novel and the author's last such work, and continued their attacks on her reform fiction. *The Athenaeum* wrote: "Four years ago, on the appearance of Mrs. Trollope's 'Factory Boy,' we entered a protest against the mode of dealing with popular questions followed in that bad book, and we set before the authoress the dangerous responsibility of such one-sided appeals to passion and prejudice." *The Spectator* accused Trollope of "taking advantage of attractive temporary circumstances" and of appealing to "vulgar prejudices and vulgar cant." Indeed, the reviewer continued, her "character and story are so obviously framed to forward some theory of the author that they come to be considered less in the light of humanities than machines."[26]

Yet in spite of this castigation at the hands of critics for handling coarse, vulgar, and inappropriate subjects, Trollope had persisted in investigating forbidden or neglected areas, and in exploring the sexual problems of her gender in Victorian society. She proved herself a serious researcher, with a strong commitment to social reform. In *Jonathan Jefferson Whitlaw* and *Michael Armstrong* she buttressed her stories with eyewitness knowledge gained on travels and arduous fact-finding trips. For the *Vicar of Wrexhill* and *Jessie Phillips* she used personal experience and contemporary pamphlets and materials as the basis for her graphic scenes. Several of these novels she had deliberately published in monthly parts, so as to reach a wide audience. In all of them, her style was sharply caustic; she gave her readers no relief, or Dickensian humor, to mitigate the bleakness of scene and story. She boldly approached sensitive issues of social justice and noted even the sexual implications of slavery, evangelical piety, and the clauses of the New Poor Law. Pointedly, she made women take the lead in improvement and rejuvenation in these novels. Throughout the next years of her already long and distinguished writing career, she would continue to dramatize the woman question with boldness and originality. Indeed, this issue, raised first in these novels of social reform, would become the central concern of her later years.

Chapter Four

Novels of Feminine Consciousness: The Strong Woman

Romance

In the nineteenth century most women accepted the prevailing definition of their proper role: marriage is the natural destiny of the sex. Despite their own deepest awareness of selfhood, even female artists were limited by such patriarchal pronouncements and found it difficult to create viable heroines who did anything more significant than marry.[1] From the beginning of her writing career, a focus on the unused potential of women had been at the heart of Trollope's work. She was among the first to write persuasively and with purpose about the role of women in the countries she described in her travel books. In her social reform fiction she used women as the vehicles of social change. But given the prevailing conventions of fiction, it was not easy to introduce strong, independent women characters into the main plot line of popular novels. Between 1833 and 1843 she experimented in Gothic and comic modes, where deviations from feminine norms of behavior would be more acceptable, and she could more easily introduce unconventional heroines.

The Abbess: A Romance (1833).   The earliest appearance of the dominant heroine is in *The Abbess*, a book written in the already established Gothic mode of Anne Radcliffe, one of Trollope's favorite authors during her young womanhood. *The Abbess* abounds in adventure, passion, intrigue, and the more specifically Gothic elements—terror, "mountains, spectral music, defenceless beauty and the Inquisition, ruined manors, vaults, pilgrims and banditti."[2] To resist the power of the Inquisition, with its hooded attendants silently removing victims to torture chambers and trumped-up heresy trials, Trollope created the Abbess, a beautiful and dignified young woman named Geraldine, really a secret Protestant, long ago forced to take the veil by her credulous and tyrannical father. While never believing in the Roman Catholic creed whatsoever, Geraldine's talents have enabled her to become superior of the convent. Most of her heroics involve the saving of defenseless young women, one a recalcitrant daughter facing imprisonment in the nunnery, and another a pregnant noblewoman in disguise. Her chief adversary is the wicked monk Isadore, who long ago had poisoned Geraldine's mother.

This kind of melodramatic material was common to the Gothic novel, and *The Abbess* is not a disappointing example of that popular genre. What was new was the courage and determination of this woman, who relies on no hero for rescue. Clearly reflecting on her own situation, Trollope wrote *The Abbess* while her hapless and bankrupt husband was ill with constant headaches, and aging rapidly. Two of her children were displaying alarming symptoms of the consumption that would eventually kill them, and another daughter was dangerously frail. As she nursed the invalids and composed the novel, it seems little wonder that her heroines emerged as remarkable for their strength.

The book was financially successful and praised by the reviewers. As the *Spectator* noted, *The Abbess* was composed by "a not unskillful bookmaker" and would "extremely well suit the wants of the ladies who have been long pining for a genuine bit of romance, much as they used to be supplied with in the days of their youth—those 'deep' times when Mrs. Radcliffe made them hide their heads under the bed-clothes, and converted every sound into a warning and every sight into a ghost."[3]

Tremordyn Cliff (1835). After her family's eviction in bankruptcy from Harrow and the nursing of several terminally ill family members, Trollope began writing yet another highly colored novel with a strong heroine, whose feeble younger brother succumbs to a nameless condition marked by severe hemorrhaging, certainly an oblique reference to the author's own present concerns about the health of her severely consumptive son Henry.

The highborn and ambitious heroine, Lady Augusta, is the oldest of seven sisters whose hope to become countess and sole possessor of her father's estate and titles is crushed by the unexpected birth of a brother. Soon afterwards, her mother dies, and, upon dismissing her governesses, Lady Augusta becomes mistress of Tremordyn Castle. Loving ascendancy, and clearly capable of mastering others, she would have made a better ruler than the soft-hearted, delicate, and somewhat effeminate rightful heir. Even her brother's eventual wife observes: "It is a pity she and her gentle brother cannot make an exchange; she would be the most lordly knight that ever buckled on a sword, and he would be . . . the very prettiest damsel in the world" (1:45-46). All Augusta's thoughts are of power and she records her frustrated ambitions from time to time in a private journal. Some of the entries focus on the discriminations attendant to being a woman, as she agonizes over her father's failure to recognize her superiority to her brother. Others inform the reader of her plans to become Countess of Gatcomb and to make her brother dependent upon her, while concealing her deep hatred of him.

She controls the upbringing of young Theodore, employing only tutors who will emphasize his softness and delicacy. When just three years remain in Theodore's minority, her father dies. Augusta now takes total command. On a trip to Italy, however, young Tremordyn is captivated by the beautiful Catherine Maxwell. When Augusta protests his attachment and planned wedding, the young earl bursts a blood vessel, and doctors predict he has not long to live. Augusta plots to continue making scenes that will hasten his death. When he does manage to marry Catherine, he almost immediately dies of an apoplexy. Augusta thereupon steals the wedding certificate and leaves Italy. The rest of the story revolves around the young widow and her attempts to prove the legality of her marriage and the claims of her child to inherit the Tremordyn estates. She is unexpectedly resourceful in preserving her son from evil gossip, poverty, and Augusta's machinations. When Augusta's schemes to disinherit the rightful heir eventually fail, a timely leap from Tremordyn Cliff ends her life and the book.

Despite its obviously melodramatic bent, the novel interests the modern reader because of its upending of the usual characterizations of men and women. The males of *Tremordyn Cliff* are either fragile, abject, or vile; powerful women hold the central focus of the plot. From now on, Trollope's heroines grow to be the formidable matches of their men—in some cases clearly out-Heroding Herod in the matter of getting the upper hand. She was herself her family's emotional and financial mainstay. How could Trollope have put her artistic energy into creating submissive women, ladies "formed of that softest, purest, and most plastic clay, of which the great majority of womankind are fabricated" (2:81-82)? Overall, the reviewers were impressed with the book, and particularly with the character of Lady Augusta. *The Athenaeum* objected only that "her picture contains one giant and a score of pigmies. . . . There is not one who for an instant divides attention with the beautiful, intriguing, fiend-like Countess." *The Spectator* called Augusta a "new Lady Macbeth."[4] Clearly, Trollope was on her way to developing a new, vital kind of heroine.

The Ward of Thorpe Combe (1841). In *The Ward of Thorpe Combe* Trollope's heroine is a homely, selfish, and cold orphan. Sophy Martin is a woman on the make, calm, self-possessed, ever watchful of her own interests, able to seize each moment for her own advantage. Although she must deal with those who are more powerful and wealthy than she, Sophy is quick to find their weak sides and turn all to her own profit. She succeeds in making herself amiable and attractive to her old uncle, by ministering to his wants and by arranging her hair and clothing to resemble those of his long-lost son, Cornelius. Indeed, as Mr. Thorpe exclaims, "I never saw a girl so like a boy" (1:20). After Mr. Thorpe's death, his will declares Sophy his heir, replacing a whole host of closer and more deserving relatives.

Once in power, Sophy makes herself comfortable by outfitting a special set of rooms for her own use, and eating lovely meals on silver service while the others eat humble fare, plainly served. She wears the family diamonds and aspires to a marriage with a neighboring lord, but in the end the rightful heir returns to claim what is his. Still, Sophy manages first to marry one of her fortune-hunting admirers and wheedles a legacy of £300 for life from the Thorpe estate. She was a most uncommon heroine for her time—unpleasant and repulsive, as the reviewers did not fail to note, yet not without interest. *John Bull* noted that Frances Trollope "has added a new creation to the stock of the novelist, and a new study to the student of human nature." And even the usually hostile *Athenaeum* admired the unusual story with its vivid portrayal of "greediness, vanity, flattery, falsehood, and the crimes to which those appetites and attributes lead."[5]

One Fault (1840). Another of Trollope's strong heroines brought her into delicate territory: the depiction of women who must endure unhappy marriages, thrown against their wills into positions of action and strife. In the early nineteenth century comparatively few novels dealt seriously with the emotional and physical problems of marriage. Most popular novels concentrated on the obstacles surrounding courtship and not on "the less attractive side of matrimony from the inside."[6] *One Fault* dramatizes a marriage from its hopeful beginning to its gradual decline and death. Isabella Wentworth weds a rich man, choosing him in accordance with the wishes of her family and her own conviction that the union is a suitable one. Gradually, serious problems develop, including Wentworth's tendency to fancy affronts, his unreasonable demands for his wife's absolute obedience, his humorlessness, and jealousy. In general, he and his young wife are incompatible in age, social status, and temperament.

The marriage fails primarily because of the husband's character and his stubborn insistence that his wife play a totally submissive role in their relationship. Isabella's resistance to such a role, although relatively quiet and undramatic, is another manifestation of Trollope's new kind of woman. At first, like many of her contemporaries, Isabella is sure that the cloud hanging over her marriage arose "from some ignorance or deficiency in herself . . . and she endeavoured to accuse herself of caprice and exigence, rather than conceive it possible that the man she so earnestly desired to believe perfect, was out of humour without a cause" (1:188-89). Gradually, the wife comes to see that the fault lay rather with her husband, "an ill-tempered man" (2:249). Often, Frances Trollope enters the narrative to stress the importance of temper in marriage. Wentworth's inflexible and humorless insistence on his own rectitude ruins the marriage. He "had not a vice, saving his ill-temper, and his overweening opinion of his own excellence" (2:191). But by the century's standards he was a "good husband." By making her heroine want more than moral scrupulousness, sobriety, and a degree of piety in her man, Trollope raised a call for a kind of marriage that would bring not only status and economic security but emotional and psychological satisfactions to women.

Outwardly, the Wentworths continue the social round of dinner parties and evening parties leaving everyone but the reader unaware of the profound discontents in their marriage. When Isabella is finally released from unhappiness by her husband's unexpected death, she turns to a young man whose temperament is radically different, stemming largely from his exceptional closeness to his mother and his correspondingly greater understanding of women's sufferings. As the author directly states: "It was the temperament that, from the moment his understanding received the idea of his mother's having to struggle with difficulties, had caused him . . . to feel for [Isabella], and for her situation, exactly the same sort of instinctive tender interest, that the generality of human beings feel for themselves" (1:79). In short, Isabella's new lover exhibits the tenderness that, at least in literature, not until D. H. Lawrence would be expected to be present in man's response to woman.

The plot of *One Fault* puts forth the thesis that female submissiveness in marriage is both wrong and dangerous. Isabella, who tries to shut her eyes to her husband's faults and remain quiet, only accelerates the disintegration of her marriage. Trollope's narrator is sure that had this Griselda-like heroine been instead "a high-spirited violent woman, . . . her liberal, gentlemanlike, and honorable husband might have been cured, after a few years struggling, of those pampered vices of temper which now neutralised or smothered all his good qualities" (2:153). Contradicting the accepted female role models of the popular social arbiters Mrs. Ellis and Mrs. Sanford, Frances Trollope here suggested that marriages might grow stronger when partners contended on equal terms and without enmity, bringing the strengths of their own personalities to bear upon their partners in a healthy balance of wills. Her novel thus offered a new pattern of conduct for nineteenth-century women.[7]

One Fault shows the reader what marriage looks like to an unhappy wife and ends with an envoi dedicated "to those for whose especial use it has been written," which was surely not totally humorous in intention. In this farewell Trollope contrasts the fates of most women in the real world with the more improbable solutions of fiction:

To all mothers and all daughters, with most kind wishes for success in all their projects; together with a friendly request that they will bear in mind one important fact; namely, that all ill-tempered men who may make large settlements, do not die at the age of twenty-six years (3:312).

Comedy

Trollope's choice of the comic mode for her next novel was in part dictated by the continuing difficulty in fitting her strong heroines into the contemporary models, those small, gentle, large-eyed, and loving women who comprised the composite Victorian heroine, both of serious and romantic fiction, and were always, in Thackeray's phrase, "pale, pious, pulmonary, crossed in love, of course." Henry Fielding, Dickens, and Thackeray had dominated the comic novel, traditionally a genre with a male hero whose daring escapades and sexual conquests would have been inappropriate for women. Despite Thackeray's own artistic appreciation of the more unconventional heroine (ten years later he created the daring Becky Sharp, although he eventually punished her for her misdeeds), he continued privately to believe that most women, as he said of Charlotte Brontë, preferred to fame or any other earthly good "some Tompkins or another to love and be in love with."[8] Readers were not accustomed to heroines who roamed on a quest for their personal fortunes. Yet Trollope herself had done just that. Seeking more latitude to present her new kind of heroine, she created the female picaresque, with a woman ready to travel anywhere if she could expand the potential of her own, defiantly middle-aged destiny.

   The Widow Barnaby (1839).   It has been persuasively argued that "the only plot that seems to be concealed in most 19th century literature by women . . . is in some sense a story of the woman's quest for self-definition."[9] In most of Trollope's early novels the strong female characters are evidence of this search. The Widow Barnaby is her first heroine to project clearly the author's own fortitude and autonomy, self-assertiveness and curiosity about the world, and to embody the significance and drama of her own strenuously active life. Always resilient following defeats, cheerfully enduring numerous transplantings, and possessing a unique capacity to exult in the moment, forgetting the past, the widow was a creation that arose from the deepest wellspring of Frances Trollope's own personality. Indeed, she brought Mrs. Barnaby back in two sequels, confessing "that with all her faults, and she has *some*, I love her dearly."[10]

   In *The Widow Barnaby* Martha Compton, a penniless but spirited young lady, attracts the attention of Mr. Barnaby, an older man and the surgeon and apothecary of Silverton. He marries her but, before long, she is left a widow, whose first thoughts are of her "independence and her wealth." Frankly delighted by her new state, she reflects that for the first time in her life "no human being existed who had any right whatever to control her" (1:150-52). Enjoying the enhanced power of her new position, Martha Barnaby is just the first of Trollope's subsequent long line of heroines who are much happier as widows than as wives. "When she learned that her dear lost husband had left her uncontrolled mistress of property to the amount of 372 pounds per annum, besides the house and furniture, the shop and all it contained, she really felt as if her power in this life were colossal and that she might roam the world either for conquest or amusement" (1:152). Selling the house and shop, Mrs. Barnaby perceives her widowhood as increasing the possibilities for mobility. She feels a new happiness that reflects the spirit of her creator: "There was an elegance and freedom . . . in thus setting off upon her travels" (1:212). In Martha Barnaby, Trollope depicted a female longing and restlessness that was soon to become an important feature of other nineteenth-century heroines, and would be a central preoccupation of her own later novels.

The widow's striking appearance and her ability to alter it on a moment's notice are elements in the book's humor. A tall, "fine woman," she has handsome features and is eager to display them to advantage. Though at first she must wear widow's weeds, she manages to convert her mourning into a striking costume:

A bonnet of bright lavender satin, extravagantly large, and fearfully thrown back, displayed a vast quantity of blonde quilling, fully planted with flowers of every hue, while a prodigious plume of drooping feathers tossed themselves to and fro with every motion of her head. . . . Her dress was of black silk, but ingeniously relieved by the introduction of as many settings off, of the same colour with her bonnet, as it was well possible to continue; so that, although in mourning, her general appearance was exceedingly shewy and gay. (1:344-45)

As she moves into middle age, she paints her face, uses hairpieces, and dresses herself boldy and in showy bright colors. No lady, she is nevertheless thoroughly a female.

The major part of this first widow book recounts Mrs. Barnaby's adventures as she aims to win another husband, even more wealthy and thus better able to help his wife to "move in society." She is first attracted to a Major Allen, but upon learning he is a card shark and swindler, turns her attention to Lord Muckleberry, who in turn trifles with the widow's affections. They exchange letters (which he saves "in an envelope endorsed 'Barnaby Papers' " (2:370), and she also treasures his notes, but only to bring a breach of promise suit, resembling the famous Bardell vs. Pickwick affair in Dickens's *Pickwick Papers*. (3:38). But alas, Mrs. Barnaby fails to make her case stick. Now bankrupt, due to the great expenditures made to catch his lordship, the widow is brought off to Fleet Prison. Eventually rescued, she marries a Mr. O'Donagough, only to be widowed once more. Again solvent through her second husband's bequests, she finally marries Major Allen, her perfect match in duplicity and adventurousness. Clearly, for Martha Barnaby O'Donagough Allen, marriage has little to do with love or feminine needs for fulfillment; husbands are necessary evils in the search for financial security and "a free entrance into good society" (1:159).

Trollope's heroine is more than the stock husband-hunting widow. Driven by ambition and aspiration to search for advancement, she is a woman who must make her way in the world and who cannot afford to let mere feelings interfere with something as momentous as marital decisions. For the widow, "the tender passion had ever been secondary in her heart to a passion for wealth and finery" (1:146). She was "firmly determined to take care of herself and make a good bargain" if she remarried (1:146). This frank attitude toward the economic realities of marriage for women, while visible earlier in the lower-class, disreputable Moll Flanders, was something new for a middle-class heroine in nineteenth-century fiction.

A tough survivor, the widow knows how to behave so as to gain the utmost in male protection, while giving nothing essential in return. Her main weapon is a mastery of the contemporary rhetoric of female delicacy: "Alas! Major Allen, there is so much weakness in the heart of a woman, that she is hardly sure for many days together how she ought to feel—we are all impulse, all soul, all sentiment,—and our destiny must ever depend upon the friends we meet in our passage through his thorny world!" [11] As the narrator notes, "there was altogether a strange mixture of worldly wisdom and of female folly in her character, for first one and then the other preponderated, as circumstances occurred" (2:187). The folly was all for show, the worldly wisdom was the real woman, securing financial independence and the ultimate in freedom before again entering marriage. Mrs. Barnaby, a strong woman who knew how to exploit the patriarchal stereotypes of female helplessness, was no doubt an invigorating kind of heroine, especially to women readers who felt restless and inhibited by strict Victorian mores. Her message was uncomplicated and direct: even while employing the necessary outward appearances, women could maintain their inner autonomy and gain the maximum of economic independence.

Reviewers at once recognized the originality of the widow's character. She was a daring liar and cheat, but her ebullience and vitality redeemed her. In making so disreputable a woman powerful and appealing, Frances Trollope had enlarged the possibilities for the nineteenth-century portrayal of the heroine. The critics paid her the ultimate compliment, an uncomfortable sense of attraction to her potentially subversive heroine and called Mrs. Barnaby "amiably disagreeable" and "delightfully disgusting." As one critic put it, trying to sum up the totality of this outrageous conception: the character was "showy, strong-willed, supple-tongued, audacious, garrulous, affected, tawdry, lynx-eyed, indomitable in her scheming, and colossal in her selfishness—*Was Für eine Frau* is the Widow Barnaby!"[12]

The Widow Married: A Sequel to the Widow Barnaby (1840). Within a year, a second widow book appeared, with illustrations by R. W. Buss, one of the prominent artists of the period. By now the widow is in Sydney, Australia, married to Major Allen. A ripe 38-years-old and pregnant, she is hoping for a girl to resemble herself and pass her likeness "down through unnumbered generations of posterity" (1:23-24). The major makes a living cheating at cards with his admirable wife's help. Eventually he is caught, necessitating a removal to England. The birth of a black-eyed little daughter gives the widow "renewed hope and renewed ambition" (1:44). She feels "as fresh in spirit, and as ready to set off again in pursuit of new plots, and new projects, as if she had never met with a disappointment in her life." In England young Patty Allen grows up, a strong-willed flirt. As part of their plan to enter "good society," the family befriends two maiden sisters, Louisa and Matilda Perkins (who provide a hilarious sub-plot), while the major establishes a kind of respectable gambling club. After the family comes close to victory (Martha and Patty are even presented at court), the major's sharking is finally observed; he is recognized and the game is up. Meanwhile, Patty has eloped with a black-whiskered Don, and she is now Madame Espartero Christinino Salvator Mundi Tornorino. At the close of the book Martha and her husband, accompanied by the children, depart for brighter fields in the United States.

In this second novel the husband-hunting focus disappears, and Trollope uses the widow's new set of adventures to expose the hypocritical, sometimes sordid realities concealed by Victorian manners. First, she satirizes some current female stereotypes, beginning with the "blushing mother" who lies awaiting the appearance of her "dear pledge of wedded love" in her "lone chamber," with fluttering and fair bosom. After this heavy dose of hyperbole, the author concludes:

"callous must be the heart, and lifeless the imagination that does not kindle at this image!" (1:23-24). She also spoofs the shy female who faints at the thought of meeting a suitor. "Poor dear girl!" exclaims her sister, opening a cupboard and taking out a small bottle of hartshorn, "it is too much for her! Smell this, my dear! Let me rub your poor temples with it." But the calculating lady, who has only been preparing herself appropriately, cries out: "Good gracious, Louisa! What are you doing to me? I shall have red patches all over my face, and my eyes will be swelled out of my head. For God's sake, take that beastly stuff away!" (3:58-59).

Married women too must defer to the popular images of female emotionalism. When the widow meets Lord Muckleberry again, she haltingly informs him she had remarried. "You must no longer call me Barnaby. Ah! my dear lord! the heart of a woman is destined from her birth to pant for an answering heart! To feelings like mine, the chill solitude of widowed loneliness was intolerable" (3:121-22). Even with husbands, women must be careful to give "gentle and generous answers (1:69-70), though Martha Barnaby O'Donagough Allen sometimes is very direct, especially over essential items like money. Although the major would have preferred "taking his lady's income under his own immediate and separate control," his wife wins out, "not being a woman to give way early, where she felt herself to be right" (1:36-37). In the polite Victorian world, as Trollope reveals, most female behavior must be an insincere charade. Thus, the widow's exploitation of the popular images of women is laudable. At least she herself never confuses the roles she plays with any inner realities.

Trollope further demonstrates that costume, too, is a prime mode of concealment and creation of new personae. When the widow prepares to meet Lord Muckleberry after many years, she contrives a dress whose hallmark, appropriately, is its indistinctness:

A sort of floating maze of drapery ought to envelop such a form as mine, in which the eye cannot justly determine where the natural material ends, and that of the dress begins—a sort of vapoury, misty, decoration should fall around the shoulders, from among which the still-handsome face should appear.

A fabrication of capes, sleeves, flounces, and furbelows "which seemed to wander, and fall, and undulate and rise agian," the dress presented the role she wished to play. The reality underneath was another thing (3:117-22). Thus language, behavior, and outward appearance all combined to conceal the truth of women's lives.

Further, Trollope exposes the fundamentally economic nature of male-female relationships in Victorian society, through a farcical description of a marriage proposal. Foxcroft (an admirer of one of the Perkins sisters) decides to ask for the lady's hand in marriage, but not before inquiring into her financial situation:

Alas! before I can throw myself at her feet, the odious trammels of the world force from me another inquiry, hardly less necessary, such unhappily is the formation of society, than the first. Before I offer my hand in marriage to your sister . . . it is absolutely necessary that I should ascertain from you whether our united incomes would amount to such a sum as I should deem sufficient for ensuring the happiness of the woman I so fondly adore.

When Louisa Perkins explains that the penniless Matilda lives entirely at her expense, Foxcroft shifts his affections on the instant:

Oh! do not, admirable Louisa! do not draw yourself away from me. . . . You know not, as yet, the wild tumult into which you have thrown my soul! Never, no never, did the tongue of woman or of angel recount a story so calculated to pierce to the very centre of a noble heart, and bind it in chains for ever. . . . How can I make known—how, by any language used by man, can I hope to explain the vehement revulsion of feeling which has taken place in my very heart of hearts since first I entered this fatal room.

Suddenly, he proposes to "the angelic woman" in front of him, "throwing himself on his knees before her, determined, as it seemed, to stake all on this bold *throw.* 'Oh! Louisa! It is yourself: Speak to me, adored Louisa! Tell me my fate in one soul-stirring word. Will you be my wife?' " (3:82 ff.). This humorous travesty of a marriage proposal is a good example of Trollope's approach throughout the book. Whenever the eloquence is most florid, the underlying sentiments are usually spurious. In such a Janus-faced society "Barnabyism" was clearly to be commended.

The Barnabys in America: or The Adventures of the Widow Wedded (1843). And indeed Trollope's heroine was so well received that the author wrote a third widow book. It was to be the most satisfying of all her novels. It was only suitable, as she noted in a little prologue to *The Barnabys in America*, that this well-beloved female character undertake "an expedition . . . to a land which all the world knows I cherish in my memory with peculiar delight" (1:2-3). In these American adventures Trollope's own life story rises close to the surface of the novel, and Mrs. Barnaby's adventures become a thinly veiled, comic version of her own experiences in America. Mrs. Barnaby is an ample-figured, red-cheeked maternal type with a love of the theatrical, who has left England in economic distress. But there the direct parallel ends. Although Trollope's honest business project had collapsed, Martha and Major Allen's fraudulent ventures in New Orleans, Philadelphia, and New York are roaring successes. Unable to outdo the American sharpies in real life, Trollope turned them over to her alter-ego and clearly enjoyed watching their duping at the skilled hands of the powerless, landless Martha Barnaby, who achieves success not through face, figure, youth, or wealth, but through the competence, resiliency, and energetic shrewdness of middle age.

The third widow book is a picaresque series of adventures. Major and Mrs. Allen arrive in America, with Patty and her new husband. Landing in New Orleans, they meet the patriotic Mrs. Beauchamp, a fortuitous circumstance which gives Mrs. Barnaby the idea of pretending to write a book of travels on the United States, in order to gain entrance to the rich, slave-holding society. Mrs. Beauchamp deplores the absence of an "out-and-out good book of travels upon the United States":

When one thinks of all the lies that have got to be contradicted, one must be a fool not to see that such a book might be made as would render the author's name as glorious throughout the Union as that of General Lafayette himself. And as to dollars! Oh my! There would be no end to the dollars as would be made by it (1:126).

Mrs. Barnaby needs no further inspiration, and immediately throws out hints that she is a famous authoress, traveling incognito the better to gather the necessary materials for a book to be called "Travels through the United States of America." The gullible Mrs. Beauchamp offers to help, for she deplores "how shamefully the United States have been abused, vilified, and belittled by all the travellers who have ever set foot in them for the purpose of writing books about us." This "regular national calamity" (1:181), has determined the lady to make the "heart in [her] bosom ready to fight for the stripes and the stars" (1:186-87). She makes only one stipulation for Mrs. Barnaby:

All I want in return is that you should portrait us out to the world for just what we really are, and that is the finest nation upon the surface of God's whole earth (1:237).

Martha is, of course, quite willing to comply: "Here come I, quite as well able to write a book as any . . . and ready enough for my own particular reasons to praise them all up to the skies. And yet, . . . I don't suppose that any living soul but themselves will believe there is a word of truth in it" (2:27-28). But for Martha Barnaby, truthfulness is not the issue:

What matters it how or in what manner a book or anything else is managed, so that one gets just exactly the thing one wants by it? It would be just as easy for me to write all truth as all lies about this queer place, and all these monstrous odd people, but wouldn't I be a fool if I did any such thing?" (2:26).

A portion of the book, now retitled *Justice Done At Last*, is finally ready, and she reads aloud from it one evening to an admiring crowd of Americans:

Nobody properly qualified to write upon this wonderful country could behold a single town, a single street, a single house, a single individual of it, for just one single half hour, without feeling all over to his very heart convinced, that not all the countries of the old world put together are worthy to compare . . . with the free-born, the free-bred, the immortal, the ten hundred thousand times more glorious country, generally called that of the "Stars and the Stripes!" (2:44).

She draws applause from an entranced audience, who naturally agree with her conclusions: "It is just the biggest and the best, and that is saying everything in two words." The major congratulates his wife for having discovered America's single most important passion, "their vanity about their country and their greatness" (2:110). The broadly humorous scene ends as Mrs. Barnaby bows "with grace and dignity, . . . slightly agitating" her perfumed pocket-hand-kerchief, and pushing "the abounding curls from her forehead," while she accepts the anticipated applause following her reading (2:42).

In the subsequent reception, however, part of the real Frances Trollope emerges from behind the swindling widow. On the pretext that she needs further information, Martha asks members of the Southern society to answer a few questions. The most probing are on slavery. How did it originate, she wonders. "You may go to your Bible for an answer," replies one of the gentlemen. "About Cain being turned black by the hand of the Lord, on purpose that he might become the father of a nation of blackymore nigger slaves" (2:66-67). And when Martha inquires what the effects of slavery were upon both the black and white population, the answer is prompt:

In the first place, it makes the only real gentlemen in the Union. In the second place, it saves the finest people upon God's earth from the abominable degradation of having no servants . . . to wait upon them. Thirdly, slavery is known . . . to be the only way in which the glorious fine sun and soil of this noblest of all countries, can be turned to the best account. Fourthly, there is no other way . . . by which such fortunes can be made in the Union . . . as to give us proper dignity in the eyes of Europe.

The widow's double-edged reply perfectly suits both her immediate audience and Trollope's readers: "Blind indeed, must those be, who cannot see the light, when it is thus admirably put before them" (2:70). And then abruptly the giddy Mrs. Barnaby reappears to inscribe the albums of the adoring ladies with appropriate phrases: "Immortal country, hail!" "Success to the Stripes and the Stars!" "The extinguisher of the Old World and the Candle or the New!" and "May lawful slavery survive as long as the sun and moon endureth!" (2:225-26).

Also part of the plot is Mr. Egerton, a young Englishman, who has come to see America himself so that he can criticize the country, whose principles he deeply disapproves. He is a monarchist, a defender of established religion, and an opponent of slavery. The love interest begins when Annie Beauchamp and Mr. Egerton are attracted to each other. Once again, the debate about the relative glories of England and America is underway, with the outcome clearly guaranteed to be the conversion of Annie.

Martha obviously can continue to hoodwink everyone as long as she wants, but the major wins too much at cards, making necessary a swift departure for New York. The family stops at Philadelphia en route, where Mrs. Allen finds the abolitionist Quakers easy prey. For them, she pretends to be writing a work castigating slavery, but she is in need of money since her husband opposes the project. The Quaker community is only too happy to subscribe in advance for a book now retitled *Slavery in the United States of America*. From there, with purses replenished, the Allens go to Saratoga, where the major swindles the swindlers and again is forced to flee. This time he disguises himself as an itinerant preacher, who fools the deadly serious members of the Needle Steeple Congregation. Thereafter the plot quickly wraps up; a slave uprising kills the Beauchamps, thus freeing Annie (who has been hidden by a black female slave) to become engaged to Mr. Egerton, just in time to join the Allens in a return to England. The latter have, of course, emerged from everything unscathed and richer by ten thousand dollars. Their schemes and swindles represent Trollope's by now all-but-blunted wish to pay the Americans back for the trials of former years. But now, all is bathed in comic light. As Mrs. Barnaby herself says of one of the major's plots, "as a jest played off to avenge, as it were, the numberless tricks which we hear of as practiced against our countrymen it is more than justifiable; and in that light, my dearest Major, it commands my warmest and most patriotic admiration" (3:285).

But the reader does not need this pointed reference, for it is clear almost from the beginning that the widow Barnaby is really a surrogate Frances Trollope. All of the latter's prejudices reappear in the book: American speech habits, female involvement in evangelical religion and revivals, spitting, and "calculating" Americans. Martha Barnaby herself has something of Trollope's chameleon personality, in her ability to rise to all occasions. Repeatedly, she saves her family from ruin, often simply by using her "acute" powers of observation and manipulation. Throughout her adventures the widow shares her creator's great capacity for enjoying life. Boredom is unknown to her: "She seldom felt anything to be tedious; she could always find or make opportunities for displaying both her mind and body to advantage; and who that does this can ever find any portion of existence fatiguing?" (1:77).

The emergence of Trollope's personality in Martha Barnaby was already well advanced in the second book, when the heroine reflects upon the causes of her success in a self-congratulatory monologue:

I do sometimes think . . . that great abilities, thorough real cleverness
I mean, is a better fortune for a girl . . . than almost any money in the
world. . . . How well I remember . . . our little town, where my father
was the rector. . . . I have managed from that time to this to get on
monstrous well. [13]

In the third widow novel Mrs. Barnaby repeatedly reflects upon her
conquests: "I do wonder sometimes where I got all my cleverness
from. There isn't many . . . that could go on as I have done . . .
always getting on, and on, and on" (1:127). In a brief imaginary
dialogue with her husband she dreams of even higher achievement:

It is not *you* who have written all these books; and if . . . a title must
and will be given, as in the case of Sir Walter and Sir Edward, it cannot
be given to *you*. . . . I know perfectly well . . . that no ladies ever are
made baronets. I know I can't be Sir Martha, foolish man, quite as well
as you do, and I know a little better, perhaps that you will never be Sir
anything. . . . Why should I not be called Lady Martha? (1:83 ff.).

Trollope, however, was not content to leave this point just part of
a dream. While Mrs. Barnaby is prevented by her sex from becoming
Sir Martha, her husband can nevertheless become Mr. Barnaby! In
a stirring tribute (and of course, also to elude the law) Major Allen
really does change his name to Barnaby "as a still further compliment" to "his ever-admired wife." In one of the century's clearest
statements of female preeminence, the major freely admits: "I can
never hope to equal you in anything" (2:243).

In the end Trollope has amused herself at everyone's expense.
Americans are fools; Englishmen are frauds. Even writers of successful books of travels are sometimes ridiculous. Yet the book is
more than farce. Against a realistic backdrop of southern slavery,
New York business swindles, earnest Philadelphia reformers, and
evangelical "saints," Trollope placed the fanciful persona of Martha
Barnaby and her enormously successful and wholesome life of deceit
and crime. But even the book's high humor could not disguise the
seriousness of Trollope's treatment of a theme that had become her
own: the superiority of women. Martha Barnaby, though a comic
character, is her clearest presentation of the strong woman.

Twelve years after the widow's final appearance, *Blackwood's Edinburgh Magazine* did a retrospective review of the achievements of
women in this "age of female novelists." There, along with Mrs.

Gore, Miss Mitford, Mrs. Gaskell, and Charlotte Brontë, Frances Trollope appeared, primarily as the creator of the "bold, buxom, daring" Mrs. Barnaby, "a work entirely after this author's heart, and at which she laboured *con amore.*" The reviewer recalled the widow, with her "coarse tricks, the coarse rouge, the transparent devices," and despite feelings of "disgust and reprobation," confessed "Mrs. Barnaby is a real kind of woman," even while wondering at "how strangely people are attracted in fiction by characters from which they cannot keep themselves sufficiently far away in real life." The writer recalled the good old days in fiction, when "our ladies were beautiful" and those who loved them were knightly, full of that "chivalrous true-love which consecrated all womankind." The critic, whose real point was the evolution of the heroine in the works of women over the last decade, located the turning point in the appearance of Jane Eyre, that "little fierce incendiary" who had turned "the world of fancy upside down," and properly included Trollope as one of the precipitators of this change.[14]

Indeed, ten years before Jane Eyre, Martha Barnaby had made her own way in a male-dominated world, struggling and advancing herself by dint of her own wits. Her life was a declaration of the rights of women. As *Blackwood's* writer noted, "Here is your true revolution. France is but one of the Western Powers; Woman is the half of the world. . . . Here is a battle which must always be going forward."[15] Trollope's widow books are a comical version of that battle, in which it is abundantly clear that even equality is too little for the peerless Martha Barnaby.

Chapter Five
Novels of Feminine Consciousness: The Marital Imperative

In her very first creative effort, a curious little poetic fiction, *The Mother's Manual* (1833), Trollope had Lady Hook instruct her daughters in the techniques of landing husbands. The author's methods of characterization and plotting would grow more subtle as her career developed, but the message remained the same until almost the end: woman's most accessible source of power came through marriage. In the fiction of this period (1840–1849), while happily marrying off the docile heroine remained the business of the main plot, Trollope developed new female characters who act out the rebellious assertiveness not expressed by the heroine or by the author. Giving over the surface of her novels to the conventional heroine, she threw her energy into creating meddling, aggressive, manipulative, shrewish fortune hunters, who struggled to control the world on their terms, conquering men even as they ostensibly submitted to them in marriage. The vitality of this important character attracted both readers and reviewers more than the main heroine, and embodied the author's deep conviction that there was quite another side to the feminine personality, full of strength and passion, qualities necessary both for woman's pleasure and survival.

The success of her Widow Barnaby books inspired Trollope to create more females with initiative. Also, in 1843, she had completed the last of her fiction of social reform, a genre which increased her own sense of influence and in which she had used women as the primary agents of enlightenment. That same year she left England to take up residence in Italy. This physical distancing enabled her to explore the position of women from a new vantage point. Over the next ten years she functioned as a skillful professional writer. Seldom a year passed without one or two new romances from her pen. The books were all written with enthusiasm and gusto;

her success as a writer was due to her ability to describe reality in a light, satiric fashion. In general, however, the books did not differ from the rather conventional love stories then on the market. She too told of young heroines seeking and accomplishing marriage. New, however, was her introduction of a variety of subplots populated by intelligent and self-willed girls, who simply did not fit into the accepted mold. While the widow Barnaby had conquered through her enterprise and loquacity, these characters added sexuality to obtain power over men. In these peripheral creations Trollope continued to develop a more congenial female character, whom she cast in a supporting, but crucial role, as villainess, siren, unhappy wife, and, most important of all, fortune hunter.

Beginnings: *Charles Chesterfield* (1841) and *The Blue Belles of England* (1842)

The first two books in which such characters appear are works overlapping from the previous period, and in general their subject matter is more literary than feminist. Taken together, *Charles Chesterfield: or the Adventures of a Youth of Genius* and *The Blue Belles of England* satirized the London literary scene. In a most unusual circumstance, both appeared simultaneously in monthly parts, between July 1840 and December 1841, in two different magazines, *The New Monthly* and *The Metropolitan Magazine*.[1] Thus Trollope continued to exploit the monthly serialization and to attack the literary conventions of her day; all the prevailing fads and especially the hypocrisy of the so-called "Moderns" became the subject of her ridicule.

The plot of *Charles Chesterfield* follows the fortunes of a young son of a substantial farmer, who unexpectedly inherits a legacy from a considerate godmother and departs for London hoping to become a brilliant literary success. "It was the world, it was London, for which he panted. Fame, renown, applause . . . such as he had heard tell of . . . as having been achieved by an individual called Sir Walter Scott, and by another named Lord Byron" (1:40). In town, he is introduced by a swindling patron to a literary coterie, including the famous critic Marchmont, who attaches himself to the naive Chesterfield, circulating him among celebrities and instructing him on the techniques of modern literature. Soon Charles becomes somewhat entangled with a Mrs. Sherbourne, a literary lady. In the third volume, disenchanted with these parasites, Charles begins to see his new friends for what they are, as Mrs. Sherbourne threatens to sue him for breach of promise, and his poetic work is rejected by an honest publisher. Finally Charles returns to the country, marries his old sweetheart, and becomes an honest clergyman, thus rejecting the lure of London's "heartless puppetshow" (2:58) and fame.

In this book Trollope focuses primarily on the critic Marchmont, whose characterization enables her to attack the inflated ideas of literary genius then in fashion. Marchmont affects long hair and an "uncovered throat" à la Byron and Shelley and drinks freely for inspiration, for, as he says, "even the mighty steam engine itself wants oil" (1:296). Always presumably too distracted to hear what is being said to him, he is admired by some who gush: "Does it not remind you of the stories we have heard of Sir Isaac Newton? Beyond all question his power of withdrawing the soul from outward objects is one of the most precious privileges which nature accords to genius" (1:171). Introducing Chesterfield to Marchmont, the artistic Mrs. Gibson calls out: "Descend! Come down! 'Tis time" (1:172).

Trollope also uses the character of Marchmont to expose the nonsense of the modern notion of "originality." Marchmont finds the only obstacle to Charles's successes is his extensive formal education. As he explains of his own background: "My grammar is mankind, my friend; my dictionary is in the clouds. The winds are my syntax, and rushing cataracts my prosody!" (1:176). Tradition is unimportant. "This pitiable reverence for antiquity is now happily passing from the earth for ever" (1:191). But the quality of Marchmont's talent becomes clear in the very first stanza of his poem "On a star seen at midnight."

> Bright candle in an everlasting stick!
>   How soothingly thy trembling rays descend
> Upon a heart from o'erwrought feeling sick,
>   Whose leaping pulses towards madness tend! (1:194)

Trollope's view of artistic inspiration had little to do with either "leaping pulses" or madness. Her position was later adopted by her novel-writing son Anthony: *"Labor omnia vincit improbus."*[2] She had but scorn for Marchmont's inflated ideas of artistic genius.

Marchmont's first assignment for Charles is to review a new book, *The Philosophy of Suicide.* When the protégé protests that the topic is itself a contradiction in terms, Marchmont uses the occasion to enunciate his philosophy of literary criticism. "Don't ever take the same side of a question as all the old fogies." Emphasize incongruity—concentrate on form ("the sparkling style"), not content. "You need not trouble yourself to say clever things." Instead, "make people stare a little . . . by saying something startling and wild." Along the way, "avoid all words and phrases which tend to give a precise and clearly-defined idea to the mind" (1:281-85). Marchmont, it turns out, is also the influential editor and reviewer of a literary magazine, the *Regenerator,* a substantial portion of which "is devoted to the passing sentence on the literary productions of the day." Influenced mainly by the name, reputation, or political principles of the authors and not the quality of their books, Marchmont takes pleasure in anonymously demolishing literary products with his "cut-and-thrust manoeuvring from behind a golden screen" (1:287).

Worse, he bluntly confesses to Chesterfield that most reviewers do not actually read the books they describe, and giving Charles his list of notes for his own forthcoming articles, he demonstrates how easy critical comment can be. One simply takes the title, uses one's prejudices, and starts:

1. *Thoughts on a Future State of Existence.*
Execrable. Bigotry. Intolerance. 19th Century. Stumbling-block in the progress of thought. To be done savagely, but jocosely.

2. *The Tyranny of Passions: or Absolution by Right Divine.*
Admirable. Courage of truth. Strength of Argument. Irresistible reasoning. First-rate talent. Commanding intellect. To be done in a high transcendental tone of enthusiasm. (3:6)

Charles wonders if "this omnipotent business of reviewing" can really be "all humbug" and chance. No, says Marchmont, all depends on knowing the author or his principles. Conservatives are always attacked, while avant-garde writers, like the author of *The Convict Footman,* are praised to the skies, with the kind of literary "hype" still familiar one hundred and forty years later. "We hail these volumes as the advent of a new era in the history of man" (3:13).

Having so long been flayed by the reviewers, Trollope enjoyed counterattacking with her completely odious creation, Marchmont.

More significant in terms of the development of her future themes was the appearance of more strong women characters, predictably cast in subsidiary plots. In her lineup she included two artistic ladies, the first the fraudulent Mrs. Gibson, "in every sense of the phrase, a woman *à prétention*" (1:224). Mrs. Gibson is hostess to all the bright lights of the day and receives "nearly the whole host of living authors (she has 47 upon her list)" (1:260). Her second distinction is her massive work illustrating *Paradise Lost*. In her sacred back parlour she collects and colors etchings, pasting them beneath the relevant sections of Milton's great epic. To depict the rebellion of the angels, for example, Mrs. Gibson uses a plate showing the breaking up of the school at Dotheboy's Hall from *Nicholas Nickleby*, an idea with which "everybody is delighted" (2:182). At the novel's end this literary hack work is "superbly bound in 43 volumes" and becomes one of Mrs. Gibson's "lions" (3:337-38).

To contrast with this female dilettante Trollope created Mrs. Sherbourne, another fanciful version of herself, a woman who lived entirely from the proceeds of her writing of popular works of fiction. "No circulating library from the Orkneys to the Land's End, dared to confess that they had not got Mrs. Sherbourne's last work; and *The Condemned One—The Entranced One—The Corrupted One—The Infernal One—The Empyrean One*—and *The Disgusting One*, and all in succession, conveyed her intensity into every village of the empire, and brought in return wherewithal to 'live and love, to dress and dream' (which in one of *Occasional Poems* she had declared ought to be the whole of woman's existence), very much to her satisfaction" (2:102). But Trollope had a more serious purpose for her character than just self-portraiture. She wanted to comment on the problems of literary women in a field managed predominantly by men. Aware of a limited talent and large needs, Mrs. Sherbourne, like so many other female writers, was forced to use personal charms to advance her career.

Her professional existence depended upon her welcoming without reserve all those who could assist her in her pursuits, either by criticism or patronage. . . . Her existence glided on through a series of small literary labours, cheered by a series, equally unbroken, of small literary flirtations, each helping forward the other by a reciprocity of influence, by no means unskillfully managed. (2:104-5)

In *Charles Chesterfield* her main efforts at flirting and flattery are expended on Marchmont. As Trollope notes: "Whenever she wished to produce an effect . . . she understood perfectly well how to make common cause between her books and her beauty, without ever permitting the one to outshine the other" (2:105). Moreover, all she does must be done without "the slightest approach to indiscretion." Yet clearly, her beauty and her literary talent were both essential to her success:

Mrs. Sherbourne would as soon have thought of putting her impassioned language, her original views on all subjects, her boasted knowledge of Italian, or any other of her manifold accomplishments upon the shelf, as her beauty. Her prose and poetry, her hands and feet, her wit and her white shoulders, her philosophy and her long ringlets, her large eyes and her little Italian vocabulary, were one and all part and parcel of herself, and one and all part and parcel of "that by which she lived." (2:190-91)

Mrs. Sherbourne uses Marchmont to get good reviews for her new play, *The Matchless Minstrel*. Never forgetting her concentration on "the *wherewithal* by which all that she most loved and liked was to be obtained" (2:204), she puts out of her mind Marchmont's distasteful ugliness and disagreeable personality, remembering only that he is "one of the omnipotent WE, and member of the secret tribunal, in whose frown there was death, and whose smile brought food, lodging, hackney-coaches, and satin gowns" (2:205). So she smiled at him and put on the necessary pretense of delicate weakness. Later, she contracts to sell him her memoirs, but again not without the prerequisite pretenses:

Oh Mr. Marchmont! You little guess what it is for one so utterly unfit to breast the storms as I am, to offer my second soul, as I may call it, for sale! To carry my sorrows and my joys to market! To ask, to urge—even such a noble mind as yours, to give me gold for turning traitor to my own precious thoughts, and laying bare my heart of hearts to all men! (2:271)

Marchmont accepts the memoirs, but reminds Mrs. Sherbourne of the secret of literary success. Someone must be found to "sing out that such a work is too improper to read" (2:277); then it will have enormous sales. Surely Trollope referred obliquely here to the unwritten good turn the critics had done in their many attacks upon the "coarseness and vulgarity" of her own novels.[3]

The Blue Belles of England, which appeared simultaneously, is another clever satire on the fashionable London literary world. The book begins as Constance Ridley comes of age and into £30,000. Even as Charles Chesterfield had wanted to win literary renown, Constance's ambition is to make personal acquaintance with those who "had acquired honourable fame" (1:24) in the arts. Through her friends the Hartleys, she contrives to get "introduced to the London world" (1:31), a favor for which she must help pay expenses. As is so often the case with Trollope's heroines, Constance has a foolish brother, Sir James. "Everything belonging to, or emanating from, the mind of the brother was little, trifling, and dwarfish. Even his faults were on a small scale" (1:23).

One of the Hartley girls, Margaretta, decides to lure Sir James into marriage. She does not love him. Indeed, since a crush at age sixteen, she tells her mother, "I have never been the victim of any tender passion whatever" (1:87). Sir James, vain and rich, is fair game to her. He, for his part, thinks himself safe. As he tells Constance, "I'll defy all the women in London, old or young, to catch me" (1:111). Margaretta is the first in what was to be a long series of aggressive but curiously attractive fortune hunters. She exploits opportunity and male vanity to win a rich husband in a "steadfastly purposed and patient" campaign (2:259). She tells her mother: "There is not a girl in London, let her advantages be what they may, who could compete with me in this charming chase. . . . He comes to me as constantly, and as naturally, for my little compliments to himself . . . as Cloe [the horse] does to the footman to be fed; and you will see, Mamma, that before long he will find out that he cannot do without them" (2:169-70). In fact, she finds Sir James "such an uncommon fool, and so utterly devoid of everything like the spirit and feeling of a man," that she considers her activities "very dull work, [and] very difficult too" (2:284).

But this side of her nature is carefully hidden as, simpering, she plays the part of the timid maiden. "She made her appearance, raised her timid eyes, averted her blushing cheek, gave her trembling hand, and performed every other part of the routine expected and required with the most irreproachable propriety of demeanour"

(2:301). Her subsequent marriage is one long exercise of tyranny over Sir James. Without power, she candidly concludes, there was nothing to "sustain her under what she felt to be a most prodigious bore." The phenomenon, the author assures the reader, "is by no means uncommon," and modestly adds: "Never, perhaps, had there been a finer example seen of a strutting, vain, and silly coxcomb, subjugated to the tyranny of an artful and ingenious wife," who just happened to be more violent, headstrong, imperious, and unreasonable than himself (3:234).[4]

Contemporary reviewers noticed that the best parts of Trollope's novels now often had to do with these determined women and their machinations. *The Spectator* wrote of *The Blue Belles*:

Mrs. Hartley and her husband-hunting daughter Margaretta, and the bragging baronet Sir James Ridley, whom that designing lady trepans into marriage, are the best-drawn characters in the novel. In the anatomizing of baser natures, Mrs. Trollope is skillful and diverting, though the amusement is of a disagreeable kind.

Properly reflecting Frances Trollope's own creative instincts, the reviewer admitted, "when the fate of the heroine alone engages the attention, the interest . . . flags."[5]

Constance, the conventional heroine, is dazzled by the fashionable literary world, whose main hostess, Lady Dart, insists "it has been the favorite object of my existence . . . to collect round me all that nature had let slip through her fingers upon us of divine" (1:120). Many of the names of those present are thinly veiled versions of celebrities from the real literary world, like Mr. Lodhart (the critic Lockhart). The center of attention is the poet Mortimer, who is surrounded by "the Blue Belles of England," admiring coteries of women who follow in the wake of successful authors (1:147). As one of the Miss Hartleys explains:

One hundred and twenty . . . sent their albums . . . beseeching that [Mortimer] would write a few original lines in his own delicious vein of poesy therein. Seventy modestly entreated that he would only vouchsafe to inscribe his name at full length on a scrap of paper . . . One hundred and three requested . . . a small lock of his hair; and fifty-two sent him poetry of their own composing. (1:179)

Many of the book's ladies have literary aspirations. Lady Dart keeps a notebook (her "museum of ideas," 2:7), and Lady Georgiana Gray-

ton is "a prodigious verse-writer" (2:40-41). Everywhere, women
are striving to advance themselves through a variety of means, either
literary or marital. Most innovative as a female character is one of
Mortimer's special friends, the unique Mrs. Gardiner-Stewart. Like
some of the book's other women, even while married to a pleasant
and polite nonentity, who appears at parties and does not interfere
with his wife's diversions, she too is searching for power and control
over men. A "very sweet woman," she surrounds herself with beautiful things—plate, linen, perfumes, and keeps "that vulgar article
called daylight" out of her rooms with silk curtains and venetian
blinds. Her house is a "palace of dainty devices" (1:230). The
drawing room is scented by "a delicate incense from Arabian gums"
and lit by tapers and decorated with flowers and "hangings of lemon-
coloured satin, gilt ornaments, and a multitude of mirrors" (2:195).
She "hated standing" (2:182), and settles herself prevailingly upon
her sofa in "an attitude exceedingly recumbent" (2:196). As the
narrator suggests, "no one living could exhibit symptoms of being
ennuyée more conspicuously than Mrs. Gardiner-Stewart" (2:181).
This lethargic pose masked an inner determination and toughness
as, with "closed eyelids" and an "air of perfect and very soft and
beautiful repose," she listens to the whispered compliments of admirers and controls the fates of many of the gentlemen who haplessly
swarm around her alluring presence. She is one of the earliest por-
trayals of the siren figure, later so masterfully developed by Anthony
Trollope in *Barchester Towers* with his Signora Neroni.

In the second volume Constance accepts the marriage proposal of
Mortimer, the poet. Soon, however, she sees him "as he really was,
artificial, vain, little-minded, and insincere" (3:101). A Mr. Fitzosborne has, instead, "so many of the higher qualities which were
wanting in her affianced husband" (3:104). To extricate herself from
this difficult position without harming others is her task in the
third volume. After an appropriate number of delays and misun-
derstandings, Constance and Fitzosborne are united. In the end
Constance has come to see what Frances Trollope set out for her
readers, the fickle shallowness of the London literary scene, both
the lionized artist and the coteries of hangers-on.

With the writing of *Charles Chesterfield* and *The Blue Belles* Trollope
embarked upon a succession of works treating the men, women,
and manners of the age. Her perception of the ludicrous and the
power of satire remained undiminished, making these works vig-

orous and popular, as she turned ever more intensely to analysis and criticism of her own society.

The Fortune Hunter

Young Love (1844).   The main interest of *Young Love* is not its conventional romantic plot, from which the author herself turns pointedly aside: "And this, gentle reader, is all the love-making between my hero and heroine with which I can favour you" (3:372). Instead, Trollope introduces Amelia Thorwald, surely one of her most unscrupulous fortune hunters. Reviewers found her "rather too much of a heartless profligate." Her maneuvers, her mock marriage, her lies, the episodes she inhabits "have something revolting about them," wrote one critic.[6] Yet once again, the real vitality of the book lies in the machinations of a fortune hunter.

Amelia goes quickly to work in the usual surroundings of country society, selecting for herself the man who possesses the most economic and social power, Alfred Dermont, "the first young man in the company, . . . the richest, and the handsomest," the one with "the greatest power of making her conspicuous by his attentions" (1:169). As in the usual situations created by Trollope, Amelia has no romantic feelings for the prey, "a horrible bore" she calls him to a female confidante: "Whether my poor shattered spirits will bear the wear and tear of his young love . . . from noon till dewy eve . . . I cannot tell" (2:9). The lack of emotional involvement is a constant with this character type. The new ingredient in Amelia is precisely her hope to marry someone she truly likes. She prefers another man, the older and more sophisticated Lord William, and gambles all on one more try at him, even while keeping the naive Alfred on a string, "a dangerous game" as her female mentor warns (2:14).

In this book Trollope uses the device of letters to get inside the real Amelia, about whom, in company, there is nothing "natural or involuntary." As the narrator pointedly notes: "Nothing can assist the development of character so effectually as the perusal of confidential epistles" (2:77). Amelia's letters are directed to an older woman who has also suffered in life, going from teaching to a "very advantageous marriage," to destitution and misery, to lady's maid, and in her final transformation, to clothes merchant. Amelia writes her sympathetic friend in confidence, "opening an aching and over-full heart" about the "insipid and wearisome boy" she will have to marry if she can "hope for nothing better" (1:88ff).

In the end Amelia abandons the sure catch to marry her choice, whom she wins by acting a scene of dramatic pathos, telling him she is being compelled to marry Alfred against her will. Later, Lord William proves to be a cad, deceiving and abandoning Amelia. But she is indomitable to the last, admitting to having been taken in, while claiming that "it is a sort of thing that no woman, let her be ever so clever, need be ashamed of" (2:299). Amelia and Lord William are divorced, and she disappears, the "latter scenes of her career" shrouded in darkness. Trollope will not punish Amelia for her valiant attempt to win both security and a man she can at least find interesting.

The Laurringtons (1844).   Dominant women abound in *The Laurringtons*: imperious mothers who rule young sons, inventive and quietly powerful maiden aunts ("Never were purses so omnipotently guinea-full, never wits so keenly inventive as theirs"),[7] and one of Trollope's most energetic fortune hunters, Charlotte Mastermann, whose name tells all the reader needs to know of her character. Charlotte, like others of this sisterhood, is a woman determined to wring security and power from an unjust and inequitable economic system. She is orphaned, a girl who has nothing and who must make the most of herself to hunt a husband and security. These women are female versions of Dickens's orphan boys who scrap and struggle to get on in the world, and Trollope certainly saw in these outsiders a variation on the theme of her own success story. Many nineteenth-century women novelists, struggling to express their own ambitions and strengths, could create only helpless and confined female characters, metaphoric madwomen in attics. Such characters are largely missing from Trollope's rich list of personae. Her fortune hunters are women who grapple with the world as it is and are an important stage in the process by which she finally gets the strong woman character out into the open, a feat achieved by few female authors of her day.[8]

Charlotte Mastermann and her brother Frank are wellborn and highly educated, handsome and talented, but with scanty funds. It is Charlotte's idea to take their seemingly inevitable story into her own hands and change it. She proposes selling what they have and placing the proceeds in funds to yield interest. As she explains to Frank: "This will enable us to give ourselves fair play for a year or two" (1:67). While people like her cousin Lady Willbury (who can afford to be willful since she has her own money) can spend their time concocting elaborate parties and fêtes in which the rich dress as peasants, Charlotte must scheme for life. After unsuccessfully trying to match Frank with Lady Willbury, she sets her own sights on the rich young Laurrington heir.

Her first strategy is to re-create her personality and lodgings in the image men have of women and their surroundings. She is, of course, sharply aware of the divergence from reality. She hated "her little home and all the ruralities that belonged to it," but knew "how the little drawing room ought to look in order to appear the chosen and dearly loved retreat of youth, beauty, fashion, and intelligence, when mingled with a little romance" (1:95). She surrounds herself with flowers, a harp, an open sketchbook, Tasso, Lamartine, Bulwer, a Book of Beauty, and "a sufficient sprinkling of morocco-cased miniatures, a gold pouncet box, filigree baskets, and the like" (1:96ff). She dons a delicate white robe and, in this appropriately chaste setting, awaits Laurrington, fully determined on "all that might and must be made of them in order to save her and her brother form utter ruin."

The enterprising Charlotte gets her man, and after her marriage immediately begins rearranging his house and possessions for her own benefit. As she explains in a letter to her brother: "You see I have found a way to do what I wanted—and so a woman of talent will ever do" (2:33). She completely dominates her husband, a fact stressed by the author several times: "Thus the penniless sister of the ruined Frank Mastermann contrived to rule with a rod . . . the heroic heart and the steadfast will of the great chieftain of the Laurrington race without encountering the slightest opposition from any one. . . . Are there no individuals among the lords of creation who can recognize their own history here?" (2:78).

Again, the fortune hunter has no emotional attachment to the man she selects. In Charlotte's case, moreover, she loathes Laurrington, telling her brother, "think you that the degradation of belonging to such an animal is no curse? " and speaking of "this detested, but absolutely necessary marriage" (3:32-33). In the third volume Charlotte's character deteriorates greatly, providing the usual moral ending of a Victorian novel. After tyrannizing her husband and his family, Charlotte tires of the game and elopes with a man she prefers. Surely, Charlotte should then have been punished by the author with some lingering disease, or madness, to be shut up in an attic perhaps. But Trollope allows Charlotte to escape without any moralizing. This obviously hardened case is last seen at the counter of a celebrated cafe in Paris, obviously enjoying herself and her life. The *Dublin Review* was unhappy with this aspect of the plot and condemned such "cold, hard, scheming wickedness, which makes the character unbearable and quite unfit . . . to be the subject of the light and gibing tone in which her schemes and adventures are narrated." But Charlotte's vitality and perseverance gained the approval of the *Athenaeum's* reviewer, who found her "as artful and fashionable a shrew as ever sold herself for an establishment and took out the sacrifice in tormenting her buyer."[9]

The Attractive Man (1846).   In *The Attractive Man* Trollope's presentation of the fortune hunter took on even larger proportions and was perceived by reviewers to have affected most of the women in the novel. The *Literary Gazette* found this a repulsive book, "especially as regards the portraiture of the females, of all ages, stations, and descriptions." Indeed, precisely because the novel was drawn by a woman writer, the reviewer was "the more dissatisfied with the degradation of the sex. There is not one specimen among the whole lot whom a man of sensitive feeling and refined taste could admire, still less love and take to be his companion for life. The bloom is off the fairest and freshest of them."[10]

The most powerful character in the book is Lucy Dalton, a girl of seventeen, another penniless orphan, who has been the heroine's companion for many years. She is the dependent who must make her way on her own. Thus she has developed through extensive reading a strong intellect, well-developed self-control, and an ability for concealment necessary, the author implies, to the powerless (1:76). From the first, Lucy longs after her rich friend's ability to make her own life story. "Ah, Miss Mary! . . . When your fancy draws pictures, you can fill them with what company you like, because it will always be in your power, you know, to say who shall and who shall not be with you. But have I the same power . . . ?" (1:76). Lucy's disadvantages are many, not the least of which is a "troublesome mother still alive who . . . was not always sober" (1:81).

Now that Mary was of age and "coming out," Lucy would no longer be able to follow her into society. Promised some money which "if carefully disposed of, might assist her in obtaining a respectable position in life," Lucy is not satisfied. She does not believe a governess's life would suit her and she determines to share Mary's position in order to marry well herself. For this task "it was necessary that her intellect should master that of Mary" (1:206). She is confident of her powers, of her "strength of mind," for her a quality more important than mere beauty. Her persistent question is that of so many nineteenth-century women in her position: "What then is to become of me?" (1:205).

Eventually, Lucy falls in love with Mary's suitor, feeling a strange sort of sympathy with him. When he too is discovered to be a fortune hunter, Lucy is undaunted. She resolves: "Let him wed money on his side, and let me wed money on mine, and then we may meet again, not hand to hand, but heart to heart, and laugh at the feeble attempts of fortune to divide us" (2:103). The attractive man of the title abides by Lucy's wishes, recognizing her "powerful mind . . . bold originality of thought, and noble superiority of spirit" (3:141). Ultimately, of course, their plot—that he marry the heiress while remaining Lucy's lover—fails, but the bold daring of Lucy, her diabolical scheming, her energy and desperation, remain with the reader long after sweet, submissive Mary Clementson is forgotten. Once again, Trollope declines to know about Lucy's ultimate fate, refusing to chastise the orphan girl who has dared so much and lost.

The Three Cousins (1847). By the time Trollope published *The Three Cousins*, reviewers were commenting on the pattern discernible in her female characters. *John Bull* noted: "Mrs. Trollope has written a great deal, and hence she sometimes copies herself; that is, we have essentially the same characters, acting from analogous motives, but externally diversified by differences of situation. . . . Her own sex she seems to have studied with profound attention, and *no living writer so keenly satirises the heartless woman of the world*, or so admirably exposes all the elaborate devices by which artificial manners are made to represent natural impulses."[11] After five years of describing such characters, the fortune hunter had become Trollope's recognized special domain.

This story concerns three cousins, ladies aged 52, 34, and 18. The eldest is Mrs. Morrison, the wife of the Bishop of Solway, who takes an interest in her young cousin, the penniless Laura Lexington. Mrs. Morrison is a "New Woman" of 1847.[12] "Every idea that was new had wonderful attraction for her. The new idiom of Carlyle,

the new colouring of Turner, the new preaching of Newman . . .
etcetera, etcetera, all excited an enthusiastic degree of interest in
her mind" (1:53). An elderly relative, Sir Joseph Lexington, with
an illegitimate son Frederick, takes a liking to young Laura. The
plot revolves around the question of how Sir Joseph will dispose of
his money. He invites Laura to his estate, gives her gifts, and outfits
her with new clothes. The third cousin, Mrs. Cobhurst, a widow
of 34, is the husband- and fortune-hunting villainess, who attaches
herself to the Lexingtons, hoping to catch Sir Joseph for herself.

Mrs. Cobhurst is a fading beauty. The reader meets her as she
undresses before a mirror, removing false tresses and artificial flowers, washing her face of its cosmetics and quickly extinguishing her
candle, "not wishing to look at herself in the glass afterwards"
(1:232-33). She tries to look like eighteen and perseveres with the
"murderous work" of flirting for a living. Once again, the lady has
little interest in the man she seeks to trap. "She was very far from
being such an extremely silly body as really to care three straws
about 'the bright vision' himself. She had gone through too many
flirtations in the course of her long military experiences . . . for
one affair more or less, . . . to touch her tranquillity" (2:160-61).
She is a woman on the make, a lone widow without protection or
assistance of any kind, but with "a brain which, if bestowed upon
a warlike monarch, might have made him the pest of his age"
(1:230). Instead, Mrs. Cobhurst is only "a restless schemer in a
little way." Such, Trollope insists, is the fate of women in the
marriage market.

The less interested young cousin Laura meanwhile falls in love
with Frederick. These potenially convenient arrangements are interrupted by the machinations of Laura's father and, of course, Mrs.
Cobhurst. When Sir Joseph dies, a will found in an old desk reveals
that Frederick is really legitimate, upon which all the cousins and
couples sort themselves out, some happily, others more resignedly.
The book's postscript belongs to Mrs. Cobhurst. Failing to trap Sir
Joseph, she has merely moved on to the next opportunity and "has
been flirting a good deal for some weeks past with a rising young
barrister, . . . endeavouring to make good her dream for a great
niece's share of the unbequeathed portion of the late Sir Joseph's
personal property" (3:347). Though she has failed to get her man,
Mrs. Cobhurst is indomitable to the last. As her creator characterizes
her, "She had great resources in an intellect, that was never for an

instant at a loss for expedients, in perseverance that was never wearied, in courage that was never daunted, and in principles that had never stood in her way upon any occasion since she reached the mature age of 21" (2:2-3).

The Lottery of Marriage (1849). Trollope turned again to a plot featuring the accomplished female sharper for her next book, *The Lottery of Marriage.* She described several ladies on the lookout, but the most prominent is clearly Cassandra de Laurie, whom Trollope elaborately introduces and parallels to the book's conventional heroine Fanny Thornton. The fortune hunter enters the stage as "a personage of very high importance in my narrative; and I would fain make her as thoroughly well known to the readers, as she is to myself" (54).[13] This is not an easy task since "there are some features of her character which it may be difficult to trace with such clearness, and at the same time such freedom from exaggeration, as may give my sketch the value of a portrait." Given the traditional passivity of heroines "in a world where initiative is too often a monopoly of the bad," the so-called "mixed female character" had always been difficult to draw.[14] Trollope had solved the problem by casting her aggressive females as comic characters and then as forturne hunters. But she wanted to draw this strong female character more roundly, make her more believable, not just a sketch but a "portrait." Cassandra is one of her most complex renderings of the fortune hunter, mainly because the author put more of herself into the character.

Cassandra's traits at first seem the same as those of her predecessors. She is clever, has studied human nature, and has learned how to make use of people for her own purposes. She is thirty, older than the conventional heroine, a fact which her creator "must not shrink from avowing" (55). Having made this confession, the author interrupts to lecture on the absurdity of "the stress which is laid upon the age of women. . . . A French author says that as long as a woman has the power of charming, she is young enough." Cassandra has no intention of falling in love with her prey and maintains an emotional distance from her "external labour" which makes her weary. As she confides to her mother, experience has given her a different perspective on the marriage game. "I certainly was a little subject to love fits some dozen years ago or so, but my intellectual constitution has improved and developed itself marvellously of late years, and I have no longer any such stuff in my thoughts" (73).

Cassandra and her mother have become accomplished artists of disguise and deception, qualities which they have learned to apply even in the small, sparse rooms they inhabit. The ladies furnish and decorate their quarters so that they seem more elegant and spacious than they really are. An entire chapter is devoted to this aspect of the fortune hunter's art, one calculated to making all she is seem more attractive to men. Indeed, when the de Lauries remove their artifices from the lodgings upon changing residence, their landlady finds the transformation as shocking "as if they had run away with the rooms themselves" (62). Cassandra is an artist of surfaces, neither ruthless nor dissipated, as many earlier renditions of this character often were.

Cassandra's closeness to her creator lies in her talent for caricature. While most young ladies of the period indulged in drawing or painting, their sketches generally were highly romantic (e.g., Jane's paintings in *Jane Eyre*) or idealized portraits (Emma's drawing of Harriet Smith in *Emma*). The heroine of Anne Brontë's *The Tenant of Wildfell Hall* has recently been called a "useful paradigm of the female artist," for her paintings are a palimpsestic art, the surface concealing the real truth, which is still, however, romantic and passionate. [15] Cassandra's talent is for drawing caricatures: fully aware of both "the peril and the profit attending this power" (56), she has effected a means for avoiding the former and enjoying the latter. She devises two volumes which are outwardly exactly similar:

But between the pages of the one were placed very pleasing, and often very accurate likenesses of her acquaintance; while, nestled within those of the other, were *the clever atrocities in which her spirit luxuriated*. Nothing was more easy than to produce the one volume or the other, according to the impression she wished to produce; and it was equally so, to insinuate the pleasing portrait of the friend to be amused, among the witty exaggerations of all the others. Or, vice versa, to enliven the comparative dullness of a gallery of nice-looking ladies and gentlemen by the occasional interpolation of some startling caricature of a well-known but distant individual. In this manner she contrived to exhibit both her talent and herself to the greatest possible advantages. (56, italics mine).

Clearly, the volume of the caustic portraits "was decidedly the most precious in the eyes of the artist." This double set is a nice symbol for Trollope's own fictional methods. The dull volumes contain the stories of the conventional heroines, while the "clever atrocities" reveal the perilous truth about society and the women who grapple with it on its own terms.

In the end Cassandra gets her man, but he proves a penniless cousin, not the real heir or the rich lord who is reserved for little Fanny Thornton, whom the author describes as lacking both the education or adventure "calculated to assist the development of her mind." Her "pretty little head" was healthy, "but many of its strongest faculties had been permitted, or rather forced, to rest in such perfect inactivity, that she had but a misty sort of notion herself that perhaps she was not quite a fool" (33). Fanny will clearly need protection. When Cassandra's marriage collapses, she is hardly upset and, significantly, when we see her at the last, she is supporting herself and her mother comfortably "by the sale of her caricatures" (419). She seems neither downcast nor foolish, and the author, far from punishing her, seems rather to be implying that even amid the present economics of society, women can survive by their own efforts. The reviewer for the *New Monthly Magazine* called Cassandra's story "one of the best worked-up sketches ever depicted even by Mrs. Trollope's clever and satirical pen," and devoted little attention to the "more sentimental love plot." *John Bull's* review called Cassandra one of the "two leading heroines of the most opposite description."[16] Clearly, Trollope was only a step away from making the "mixed female character" the heroine of the main plot.

The Unhappy Wife: *The Young Countess, or Love and Jealousy* (1848), and *Town and Country* (1848)

Two more novels conclude this stage of Trollope's development of the strong heroine, and both are devoted in different ways to accounts of unhappy marriages. Both feature enterprising women who rise above the conditions of their unfortunate unions. The young countess of the title is widowed and finds the death of her old and boring husband a release. Nevertheless, she wishes to observe the proprieties, and spends a year of mourning at a ruined old castle which, to beguile the time, she decides to restore, even re-creating its old dungeon in faithful detail. Lonely, she invites the penniless orphan Caroline de Marfeld to stay with her. Soon the Countess decides to make her protégée a permanent resident of the castle and sets up a fund for her. Anticipating a theme she would soon develop more fully, Trollope thus has her heroine seek out a friend of her own sex. She pointedly explains the countess's need in a long aside to the reader. Her heroine, she writes, needs "a dear, faithful, intimate friend, of her own sex, before whom all ceremony might be banished, every thought revealed, and with whom every project might be discussed before it was brought forward to meet the light of day" (1:49).

When the castle is complete, the countess invites a party of guests, one of whom is Alfred de Hermanstadt, with whom she falls passionately (and jealously) in love. When she suspects he loves Caroline, she locks him up in her newly built dungeon. In time the countess regrets her actions, endows an abbey of nuns, and makes Alfred her heir on condition that he marry Caroline. Fourteen years later, the reader learns that the countess has become the abbess and, in the last scene of the novel, she is reconciled with the others as she visits the dungeon in which she had imprisoned Alfred. Despite the highly colored melodrama of this somewhat ridiculous plot, the novel nevertheless features a heroine who finally finds both power and peace on her own, the real world offering no other simple possibilities.

Town and Country, in its narrative technique, also looks ahead to the novels of Trollope's last period. The book features a narrator with a heavily female voice, speaking on behalf of women in oppressive marriages (3:24-25) and, more important, uses letters and extracts from journals in order to get inside the thinking of the women, especially the heroine. Harriet's mother opens her heart in letters to "the earliest friend of her youth, from whom her marriage had separated her." Harriet herself keeps a journal, "an extract or two" from which "will throw more light upon the subject than any narrative" (1:41-42).

Harriet undertakes a May-December union with a man thirty years her senior, not unlike Dorothea's marriage to Casaubon in George Eliot's *Middlemarch* some thirty years later. Mr. Cuthbert appeals to Harriet as a source of knowledge and power. She is proud that he has found her "neither too young, too ignorant, nor too silly for him to converse with" (1:45). Attracted to him because he treats her as an equal and favors her with intelligent conversation, she marries him, to her subsequent regret. But her thirst for enlarged experience and broader horizons is analogous to that of the unscrupulous fortune hunters of this period. Not until Trollope's late novels would she give her readers heroines who found power within themselves and not in the men they successfully or unsuccessfully hunted, or accepted to their ultimate distress.

Other Works of the Period 1840–1848

In 1847 Trollope departed from her customary subject matter to attempt a topic then extremely popular, the anti-Jesuit novel. *Father Eustace: A Tale of the Jesuits* (1847) mingles clerical themes and intrigues with her usual broad delineation of modern life and the unhappy marriage plot she had so often treated. Lady Sarah finds that her husband, "instead of the bright, highly gifted being she had imagined him," was "a stern, narrow-minded bigot, the abject slave of the [Jesuit] community" (1:5-6). When he dies, Lady Sarah feels only "exceeding happiness and undeniable relief," like many of the author's other women. In the main, however, the book does not focus on this problem, but rather on those issues popular since John Henry Newman's conversion to Catholicism and the hysterical alarm that swept England following the restoration of the Catholic Episcopacy to that country.

"No Popery" had been a potent watchword for Englishmen for centuries, and the Jesuits were a specially hated group.[17] The Catholic Emancipation Act of 1829, while removing most religious restrictions, had contained the curious clause banishing all Jesuits from the British Isles. Trollope attempted to capitalize on this feeling in her sinister depiction of the Society which had acquired the admirable skill of "reigning not over the bodies, but over the souls of men" (2:98). Repeatedly, she entered the narrative to rail against the vile purposes of this organization which cheated men "out of the reasonable guidance of their own souls, for the purpose of converting them into the tools of an ambitious faction." (2:100-1). In attacking the Society of Jesus Trollope portrayed its members as mindless slaves and the embodiment of evil.

The main plot concerns the scheme of the Jesuits to obtain the large estates of Juliana de Morley, daughter and heiress of that staunch Roman Catholic father and the Protestant Lady Sarah. Father Eustace, disguised as Edward Stormont, a young, handsome, and fascinating man, is dispatched to the neighborhood to win over Juliana to Catholicism and thereafter bestow her properties on the Jesuits. As the Superior of the Order notes, "the painful aid of money is often and absolutely necessary. The brethren must live; for despite their high calling, they are as yet but men" (1:180). Unfortunately, Juliana and Edward fall in love, which provides some exciting moments leading to the disclosure of Father Eustace's true identity. He returns to Rome, and after her shock and subsequent illness, Juliana recovers to live single to old age, having returned to Protestantism. Ultimately she settles her property on a half brother. At the novel's end an aged beggar approaches; it is Eustace, who has renounced popery and returned to England, only to expire at Juliana's feet. The extraordinary, far-fetched story was not one suited to Trollope's best talents and firm practical mind. Indeed, she was never less herself than in this gloomy novel, whose theme focuses on "the struggle between religion, obedience, and passion.[18]

Finally, notice must be made of a little cluster of travel books which she interspersed with her popular fiction during this period. Although now at an age when extensive travel was becoming more difficult (in 1849 Frances Trollope would turn 70), the lure of this genre was inescapable. In the midst of other works concentrating on women and their problems, she returned three times to the subject of travel, whose sense of freedom and exhilaration had always been her deepest joy. *The Robertses on Their Travels*, serialized and published in 1846, had as its own object the satirizing of certain classes of English tourists. Since she was herself so often a traveler, the ridicule was gentle and good-humored. The writing was sparkling, and the anecdotes amusing. The book sold well, for many reviewers disputed her assertion that she had changed sufficient details so as to prevent identification of the originals, and many professed to recognize "some of the real travelers in the pages of this popular book, full of "great drollery and liveliness."[19]

Completion of the book obviously stirred up old memories and almost at once she set off on a tour of the Tyrol, Bohemia, and Silesia. She utilizes these experiences to produce her last book specifically on travel descriptions, *Travel and Travellers* (1846), sketches on random subjects, from the cold water cure of German resorts to astounding sights like King Ludwig's Valhalla on the Danube, and assorted exciting narratives of murders and contraband trade. The book is primarily interesting for its articulation of what travel had meant to Frances Trollope. Always willing to pay "the trifling exertion which it requires to leave your bed a little before you are quite tired of it," she had eagerly welcomed the "long days of wandering enjoyment" her spartan habits earned, and she bragged that she could "go farther and see more within a given space of time than most people" (2:69-70).

Although in all the rest of her writings Trollope had shown no marked evidence of religious commitments, the discussion of her travels in this work evoked from her a quasi-theological statement. As she looked over "the pleasantly varied surface of our beautiful earth," she noted: "It is good for us all to know how bounteous the God of nature has been in decorating the habitation in which he has ordained that man shall dwell during his threescore and ten years of mortal life; it is good that we should be told of it, if accident prevents our full acquaintance with the fact by means of our own experience" (2:293-94). She had spent many years viewing and describing the world to others. In the end she had herself been the greatest beneficiary. As she described the effects of the rising sun in many countries, its gradual illumination and incredible rose-colored light (1:50ff.), she greeted each day of her traveling life as a never-ending search for "fresh fields and pastures new" (2:69-70).

It was, perhaps, this casual rumination on the theme of travel that prompted her to return once more to the American scene for a novel, *The Old World and The New* (1849). The plot is flawed, containing some of her most extraordinary melodrama. She sets the bulk of the tale in the Cincinnati area to which the Stormonts and their cousin Katherine Smith have been forced by financial problems to emigrate. Katherine, in whom the love interest centers, has parted from her wealthy English suitor, Mr. Warburton, under unpleasant circumstances. In the second volume an American Indian named Oranego grows embarrassingly fond of Katherine; in the third volume he reveals himself to be the now-repentant Mr. Warburton. The reader is asked to believe that a refined Englishman could have masqueraded for several months as an Indian before the eyes of his ex-fiancée unsuspected and undiscovered!

Even more surprisingly, the novel is friendly in spirit to the United States. Of course, the old objections reappear—spitting, the nasal twang, slavery, evangelicalism, and pretentious authors, but the satire is blunted. Despite the usual English-American debate (this time between Katherine and a female American friend), the Stormonts do finally stay in the new world. It was an uncharacteristically benevolent resolution to the rather stormy relationship Trollope had enjoyed with the country that had helped to establish her reputation.

Shortly thereafter, she finished her second novel of this her seventieth year, *Petticoat Government* (1849), a romantic story whose themes and situations usher in the final period of her writing career. She was now ready to move on to write a singular group of novels praising the accomplishments of strong, independent women. Having forged her own destiny, she took satisfaction in thus spinning more stories of woman's indomitable soul.

Chapter Six

Novels of Feminine Consciousness: The Independent Woman

Beginnings

In the last period of her writing career (1850-1856) Trollope scrapped all subterfuge and allowed her strong, free-spirited women to function as heroines of the main plot. They appear as happy, self-sufficient, often older women who get along beautifully on their own. Their most frequent sources of distress are the demands of unreasonable fathers or the oppressions of weak and worthless husbands. As they achieve their variety of victories, they defiantly disregard the social and economic imperatives to marry, around which so many middle-class Victorian ladies shaped their lives.

Petticoat Government (1850).   Appropriately enough, the series begins with a story of female self-rule in *Petticoat Government*. A wealthy ward in Chancery is sent to the charge of her two maiden aunts, who struggle for the exclusive right to guard the profitable heiress. A compromise is reached, and the girl spends six months with each aunt. But these female communities abound in suspicion and squabbling. The spinster aunts (who secretly wish to be married) are only interested in their niece for her money. Finally the young heroine marries her cousin, son of another long-lost aunt, and the three form their own community far away from England.

The plot is predictable, and while there is talk throughout about women living satisfactorily without marriage, the arrangements the reader sees are all failures. Nevertheless, this novel ushers in a series of major heroines who realize their true indentities aside from marriage and, in some cases, primarily in the company of other women. In these late books the mixed female character, who appeared as comical or deviant before, now achieves her apotheosis as the clever woman whose essential self is unengaged by relationships with men.

Second Love, or Beauty and Intellect (1851).   *Second Love* is a
novel whose plot abounds not in love, but in unhappy marriages.
Some characters wed for the wrong reasons, both emotional and
financial, and others are shown struggling to cope with unhappy
unions, like Mrs. Selcroft, whose situation is the one Frances Trollope most often depicted in these late novels. "The sworn-to-be-
obedient wife of a man who often required the practice of such a
faculty in his helpmate," Mrs. Selcroft kept the knowledge of her
husband's inferiority hidden in her bosom, as the narrator pointedly
comments, "poor lady, as carefully concealed in her heart, as an
incendiary keeps his dark lantern in his bosom" (1:134-35). Her
daughter Lucy is franker and more independent, "exceedingly clever,
and not only very capable of taking care of herself, but moreover
of a disposition which might make it difficult for any one else to
take care of her effectually" (1:63). She is an intellectual girl, unwilling "to delude herself into the belief that she could love [her
father] as sincerely as she honoured her mother" (1:79-80). Not
surprisingly, her father finds her more difficult to manage than her
mother.

Throughout the novel, the narrator (clearly speaking in Trollope's
voice) pities the mother for her unshakable belief in wifely sub-
mission and praises Lucy for resisting her father's tyrannical and
unjust commands. Her plucky skirmishes with her father bring out
a pointed moral: men who "have the happiness of possessing a good
and affectionate daughter, will do well to content themselves with
the blessing, while they carefully avoid the dangerous attempt of
endeavouring to convert her into a hood-winked slave. It is just
possible that occasionally such a plan may answer with a wife, but
with a daughter, unless she happen to be an idiot, NEVER" (2:229).
Trollope's words and the logic of her plot undermined the Victorian
idea that women must blindly obey the men in their lives. At this
novel's conclusion those who resist throughout are suitably rewarded
with the demise or departure of offending husbands or fathers.

Triumphant Women

Mrs. Mathews, or Family Mysteries (1851).   *Mrs. Mathews* begins as the fifty-year-old Mary King looks back on her life and
considers the ideas and passions she has outgrown. First, she no
longer believes that women's best years are those of their youth.

She writes: "I am quite conscious . . . of being in the very highest prime and vigour of existence. When I was younger, I was less so" (2:1ff.). More important, she has dispensed with the need for romantic love and marriage. Tough and independent, she exults in her maturity and the free spirit of her singleness, even as her elderly father worries about what will become of his daughter after his death. Strongly convinced "that men only were capable of taking care of the money concerns of a family," he pressures his daughter to marry his old friend, Mr. Mathews. Protective and patriarchal, he wonders what will she do about signing the rent receipts, ordering the wine, and repairing the drains of the home pastures. Even more important, "And oh Mary! Mary! Who will sit at the side of the fire with you through the long winter evenings?" (1:37-38). Surely, he reasons, a woman needs a man for companionship above all.

Complying with his wishes, the clear-headed Mary weds, but not without strong feelings of oppression: "She did not like the idea of belonging to any man" (1:46). She negotiates a marriage settlement that will preserve much of her wonted independence, insisting on a separate allowance, the right to dispose of her own property, and the privacy of a section of the house for her own use (1:114-15). Despite these provisions, she soon finds all her worst apprehensions about marriage correct. After her father's death, Mr. Mathews shows his true colors, becomes belligerent and masterful, and in general throws Mary's happy and orderly life into turmoil. Finally, after a series of singular complications, Mrs. Mathews prevails and regains her independence. After making a will in her favor, Mr. Mathews accommodatingly dies. This easy resolution to all the heroine's difficulties should not obscure the lesson of this remarkable novel. In marriage Mary must struggle to obtain her rightful position and belongings. In the single life lay a power women had as yet not discovered.

In *Mrs. Mathews* Trollope succeeded in making a totally unromantic heroine the focus of a popular novel. A sturdy, sensible, resourceful woman, Mary King Mathews is a plain heroine who, unlike Charlotte Brontë's Jane Eyre and Lucy Snowe, finds no dashing, erotic Rochester or fascinating Paul Emanuel. Mrs. Mathews must cope with a marriage to a selfish, grasping old bachelor whom she does not love. The focus in this unusual novel is the struggle between the sexes—not a romantic one like the clashes described by the Brontë's, but a life-and-death competition between rivals for

property and the rights of inheritance, which ends not in reconcil-
iation or compromise, but with the destruction of the male and the
triumphal coming into her own of the single female.

Uncle Walter: A Novel (1853).   In the following year Trollope
published *Uncle Walter* whose plot revolves once again around the
difficulties of women in achieving satisfactory marriages given the
conventions of the time. Uncle Walter is an eccentric, but kind-
hearted bachelor of seventy, who returns home from Australia to
take possession of his patrimonial estate. He has been a naturalist
and sheep farmer, and keeps a boa constrictor for a pet. He is big,
bluff, hearty, and direct, in contrast to his straitlaced clergyman
brother, rector of a fashionable church in London. Walter becomes
attached to his niece Kate and is sympathetic to her situation, as
she resists her family's efforts to marry her off to the rich but foolish
Lord Goldstable, who is being pursued by a clever and fascinating
widow, Mrs. Fitzjames. Kate is another of Trollope's disobedient
daughters, who braves the difficulties of "opposing both father and
mother with such resolute firmness, as must oblige them to abandon
their hopes of making her a peeress" (1:293-94). Through Walter's
intervention, Kate marries a man more her intellectual equal, and
Walter makes everyone happy by settling all his money on her.

The intrigues of the designing Mrs. Fitzjames provide the novel
with a focus complimentary to that of the main plot. She is one of
Trollope's most outrageous fortune hunters, primarily because she
is already the mistress of another man. She exhibits many of the
characteristics seen before. After encounters with Lord Goldstable,
she is "exceedingly fatigued" and "dreadfully tired and languid"
(2:100). For her, all the "mysteries of lovemaking" are really just
another business transaction, and she has even calculated "in nu-
merical proportion" the respective values of all the little occurrences
of life, relative to the great task of catching a man. Supposing the
sum of 1000 to represent any given conquest, Mrs. Fitzjames allots
values to dress (100), "hair hanging in disorder (nicely arranged)"
(50), being caught reading "if the chase be literary" (25), being
seen at early Church "if he be a Puseyite" (77), a picnic (50), with
a storm (75), with a moon and dancing (150), and so on. Surely
Mrs. Fitzjames is an early type of the managerial woman in the
field of fortune hunting. None of her sisters had so totally com-
puterized the marriage market and made the hunt for a husband so
like the economic transaction it actually was (3:128ff.).

Indeed, this subplot is strongly related to the story of Uncle Walter and Kate. As the innocent outsider, Walter is outraged to find that financial considerations have prompted Kate's parents to force her to marry a rich man. Walter repeatedly speaks frank truths; he labels their actions "coercing the affections of their daughter" in order to gain the opportunity of "selling her." They have turned marriage into something only a little short of prostitution. Trollope used this story to expose the insincerity of polite language. She argues that inflated rhetoric was the facade erected by a selfish world to conceal its sordid intentions. "The key to this language is simply putting words indicative of the generous, the noble, and the great, in order to express thoughts shabby, dirty, and little" (1:133). Many reviewers were startled by the brutal frankness of this novel. One complained that "a future historian of England might fairly conclude that in the first half of the 19th century all the mothers of England were hireling match-makers," and another that the novel was written "with more than her usual coarseness and bad taste."[1]

By now, reviewers had begun to see Trollope's works as falling into a pattern, as far as her female characters were concerned. The *Athenaeum* instantly connected Mrs. Fitzjames not only with the author's previous fortune hunters ("The volumes before us introduce the reader to one more—and probably the coarsest—of Mrs. Trollope's coarse, unscrupulous scheming widows."), but with her earlier widow Barnaby, professing to see an artistic relationship between the two; but "Mrs. General Fitzjames is by no means so funny a companion as Mrs. Barnaby, while she is much more objectionable." The reviewer concluded with the by now inevitable question: "Now, we put it to Mrs. Trollope whether such are the fitting materials, and the fitting *dramatis personae* to be offered as the elements of light fiction, under the guarantee of a lady's penmanship, for the entertainment of her sex." *John Bull*, professing to see a moral message in the character, was more accepting, yet drew the connection nevertheless: "We have no fault to find with the severe caricature she draws of adventuresses and parvenues,—which by the way, are . . . decidedly her forte, from Mrs. Barnaby and her hopeful Patty, down to Mrs. Fitzjames."[2] Clearly, the portraits of strong females had become Trollope's trademark.

The Young Heiress (1853).   Her next novel, *The Young Heiress,* is a distinctly inferior, sentimental story of love and murder, with an outrageously improbable plot. The heroine, Sarah Lambert, for

many years the mistress of the turbulent ruffian, Mr. Rixley, is
rudely cast aside when he decides to remarry upon his wife's death.
He offers Sarah the job of housekeeper, a position she accepts with
surprising passivity. She has no other choice if she hopes to protect
her illegitimate daughter. Later, when Rixley dies under suspicious
circumstances, Sarah's son William is accused of murder. Now the
strong women of the plot swing into action. Sarah sets off in search
of William (who has fled, reportedly joining the navy), while Helen
(Rixley's daughter) stays on to manage her father's estate. At age
seventeen, in businesslike fashion, she controls the large holdings
so well that she can buy a commission for her half brother, all the
while fending off a number of greedy suitors.

When Sarah learns William has enlisted in a regiment bound for
the Cape of Good Hope, she follows him undaunted, and her search
takes her all the way to India. Trollope saves the surprise until the
last. Sarah dies in India, leaving behind a confession that she had
poisoned Rixley. Thus, in a single stroke, she saves her son and
publishes her long-treasured revenge. The narrator comments on
Sarah's "very strong and resolute power of self-control," seeing it
as a particular asset for women: "This sort of passive power often
very effectually supplies their want of strength, both moral and
physical in other respects" (1:110).

The Life and Adventures of a Clever Woman (1854). *The Life
and Adventures of a Clever Woman* brought Trollope's long focus on
the feminine consciousness to the forefront. Charlotte Morris is
surely one of her most confident and resourceful heroines; motherless
and headstrong, at age seventeen she is ready to leave her protective
home and its confining disciplines for London, where her rich father
plans to introduce her to society. In her earlier novels Trollope had
frequently experimented with using journals to capture the authentic
voices of her heroines. In none of them, however, did she sustain
the device for more than a chapter or two. In this book, however,
Charlotte's daily journal runs throughout, and she uses it to analyze
herself, her new friends and acquaintances, and her world, with
remarkably clear-headed and dispassionate observation. She tells all
to her journal: her follies as well as her triumphs. Calmly, she
appraises her physical assets ("not, perhaps, absolutely beautiful")
and her ultimate goal, to get herself recognized as "the possessor
of fortune, fashion, and talent" (1:99), and second, to win "lifelong enjoyment of admiration, influence, and renown."

Although marriage is not her immediate aim, she fully recognizes its importance in the social world. Her first meeting with her future spouse, as described in her journal, is singularly unromantic: "Mr. Cornelius Folkstone is not, in my opinion at least, at all a sort of person to fall in love with at first sight" (1:104). Still, she will marry him because she needs to avoid the stigma of being called "a disappointed old maid" (2:190). Her marriage is a disaster, and once the ceremony is over, Mr. Folkstone behaves like Mr. Mathews. Confident that the law will support him, he boasts openly, "What belongs to my wife, is mine; what belongs to me, is my own" (3:127). He tries to win his wife's confidence with a mixture of "kisses and coaxing," but Charlotte is neither deceived nor enraptured: "Did he really think that I would welcome his enchanting caresses one moment, and borrow a little money from my father for him the next? Let him go on—I am quite ready for him. . . . I have always thought and felt that I was not quite an ordinary character" (3:228). Once again, the battle of the sexes is underway and Charlotte is ready: "Poor man! He has met with one too powerful both in mind and position for him to cope with!" (3:229).

Folkstone goes farther than most of Trollope's oppressive husbands. Discarding all pretenses, he locks his wife up, "keeping her upon bread and water till she obeyed his commands" (3:244). Charlotte is unimpressed. Her sole regret is her inability to record these exciting events in her journal. Eventually released, she hangs on until her husband accommodates her by dying. But unlike some of Trollope's earlier heroines, Charlotte decides never to marry again, despite receiving two apparently good offers. At last the widowed woman can enjoy the state of happy singleness society denies to the unmarried girl. Triumphant, she records her hard-won wisdom in her journal, noting that fathers and husbands can easily be managed, "if women would but set their sights a little more steadily to work upon the business. My own case seems to me to furnish a very fair specimen of what may be done by a little forethought and good management" (2:179).

Gertrude, or Family Pride (1855).   The mother of the heroine of *Gertrude* is another lady who must cope with an unsuccessful marriage. Having recognized that "her husband was a pompous fool, incapable of acting from rational motives; incapable of forming a rational opinion; and pretty nearly incapable of uttering a rational word," she resolves, with "steady, quiet perseverance," to make the

best of life with "one of the dullest men that ever lived as a husband
and companion" (1:29-30). Perhaps, she reasons with practical wisdom, far worse would have been to have married "a man who, with
less of dullness, had a greater propensity to interfere with the opinions of his wife and who might have interfered more fatally still
with the occupation of her time" (1:42-43). Eventually she discovers
the great truth that Trollope's women always come to: "her only
resource against something very like despair must be sought in
herself" (1:44). Like Mrs. Mathews, she furnishes her own apartments according to her own taste and makes constant additions to
her fine old library. She also bears a daughter who provides her with
the happiness she has not found in marriage. Her only fear is "that
the intellect of her child might resemble that of its father" (1:43).
When she dies, a close female friend becomes young Gertrude's
companion. For women, motherhood and friendship are life's only
unalloyed pleasures. With this novel Trollope's interest in depicting
the female community has begun.

Sisterhood: *Fashionable Life*: or *Paris and London* (1856)

Trollope's last heroine, Clara Holmwood, is another woman on
her own. Taught by a schoolmaster. not a governess, her education,
"a very strange one," had "led her considerably beyond the limits
usually fixed, as the *ne plus ultra* of female education" (1:74). Im-
pervious to social pressures that she join the smart set, she will
accept as a close friend only a penniless old maiden aunt. In a plot
similar to that of *Mrs. Mathews*, Clara's dying father worries about
his daughter's future and is anxious that she find a suitable husband
before he dies. Without her knowledge or consent, he appoints the
odious sycophant Dr. Brixbourg as her guardian. Mr. Holmwood,
"like all other discreet men of business . . . was not, nor ever had
been, in the habit of talking to the ladies of his family concerning
his financial affairs, either private or commercial" (1:28). When he
dies in Clara's nineteenth year, he leaves her £100,000, but she
must live the remaining two years of her minority with the Brixbourg family. Like many of her creator's heroines, she resolves to
endure this trial patiently, but not without first making formal
arrangements about her rights. Aunt Sarah must stay with her,
along with her schoolmaster, for she resolves to continue her studies

in Latin, French, and English (1:74). Her only regret is that she has never studied the law, an omission that has left her unsure about Dr. Brixbourg's rights to compel her to obey his wishes. Before long a young man falls in love with Clara, not with her beauty but, as the author notes, with "the tone and quality of her mind" (1:109). Henry Hamilton, however, is too noble to pursue a girl of large fortune and sails for Australia to forget the one he loves. His departure leaves Clara free to face the question so many of Trollope's heroines encountered. What will she do with herself? How shall she shape the unknown future that lies before her?

Characteristically, her first thought is not of marriage but a profession. "Had I been persuaded into believing that I possessed a talent for painting, or for sculpture, or for music, or for astronomy, I might have amused my life, by fancying that I was making progress towards something desirable, but never having been conscious of possessing any talent at all, my existence must, of necessity, be a very shapeless one" (1:199). Yet, "conscious of an elastic spring within her which, if one scheme of existence failed, would give her energy to try another" (1:200), she turns, like her creator before her, to the next resource—traveling!

Indeed, she sets out cheerfully, perhaps too happily for the conventional heroine who has just lost her lover. The author needs to explain such feelings to readers who expected that the girl would languish: "That this state of mind was in her case reasonable, can scarcely be denied." Yet, not "every young girl as abruptly disappointed in the hopes of an apparently well-placed attachment, as she had been, could, or should, be expected to bear it so well." The generalization that follows is intended for Trollope's female readers: "There is probably no very reasonable hope of mending the matter; but as society is now constituted, the happiness of English women seems to depend too much upon the *accident* of being married, or not married" (1:197-98).

Clara certainly does not let her happiness depend on Henry Hamilton. Coming of age, she leaves the home of her odious guardian and goes to Paris, where she once again negotiates suitable living arrangements, without reference to marriage. When she meets Lady Amelia Wharton, who is poor but has good social connections, Clara decides to set up housekeeping with her friend and, of course, Aunt Sarah. Her proposal is quite businesslike: "What say you to our entering into partnership together for a month or two?" (1:213).

Pooling their resources efficiently, the women arrange to keep house together for the ensuing winter at least. Lady Amelia is quite contented with these arrangements and tells her seventeen-year-old daughter, Annie, who will also be a member of the group, "our present mode of life certainly appears likely to be very agreeable, and we should be sadly silly to destroy our enjoyment of it, by perpetually dwelling on its possible termination" (1:233).

The women get along without struggle or suspicions of one another, and their establishment is soon "as celebrated for . . . hospitality as for . . . elegance" (1:235). Indeed, "in all that passed between Lady Amelia Wharton and Clara Holmwood concerning their partnership establishment, it would be difficult for the most captious fault-finder to name any point upon which either of them could have been found wanting, either in genuine liberality of feeling, or in the unobtrusive and graceful expression of it" (1:236).

The women enjoy one another's company, even while "each was so essentially different from the others" (1:247). Aunt Sarah is "gentle, quiet, peaceful" (1:247). Annie Wharton, a "high born, graceful little beauty, contrived to animate and embellish the existence of the insignificant old maid" (1:247). Trollope's picture is one of shared happiness and considerable "freedom from social slavery" (1:275). Lady Amelia, for her part, is not at all anxious to see her daughter married off. "Marriages, they say," she explains, "are made in heaven; and though I am not sure that this is part of my faith, I am greatly inclined to think that the less busy we make ourselves about it on earth, the better. It will come when it will come" (1:277). The statement has a tone of resignation. The reader knows nothing of Lady Amelia's own marriage besides her lonely and penniless state. Her reluctance to hurry her daughter into uncertainties is understandable, but surely at odds with fictional depictions of Victorian mothers.

Soon the author is calling the ladies "partners in the firm of Wharton and Holmwood" (1:277-78), a business venture whose goal is not financial gain but rather the "very considerably increased enjoyment of each, and all, of the fair ladies of whom the family was composed." The arrangement, unlike marriage, was one in which one might amuse oneself or withdraw at will. As Trollope pointedly notes: "Perhaps of all the goods the gods can give, the most precious is freedom of will and action" (1:289). In describing the living arrangements to her old schoolmaster, Clara praises above all "the sister-like terms" under which the women live together (2:226).

In the second volume Annie Wharton does become attached to a young man, Victor Dormont. So that they can marry, Clara settles some money on her. At once the women plan to take the young couple into their circle. "Why should they not live with us here?" (2:265). Upon the agreement of all the women, they give up their third drawing room to the couple. As Clara observes; "You and your daughter, and I and my aunt, though not particularly likely from our very different portions in life to think and feel alike, have formed, since we have been together, a very happy family; and I much doubt if, in any matters of domestic arrangement, we should be likely to differ" (2:271). Thus, "none of those tearful separations occurred which will often cause a parting bride to sigh, even at the moment when the dearest wish of her heart is fulfilled." (2:277).

When Victor's financial speculations fail, he conveniently commits suicide. Fortunately, Annie has had a baby and thus, "the strongest feeling of her nature, *maternal love*" will save her (3:153). Since he had also secretly involved Clara's money in his schemes, she must return to England penniless, where a returned Henry Hamilton, who has inherited £400 a year, can now marry her. Eventually she gets her fortune back, and everyone lives happily ever after. All this action, however, takes place in the last four chapters of volume 3 and is clearly not the part of the novel upon which Trollope lavished her closest attention. The bulk of her story was a paean of praise for the pleasure and power of sisterhood.

With this novel, her thirty-fourth since she had begun a writing life at fifty-three, Trollope ended her career, giving artistic expression to a vision of female independence and sisterhood that stands out prominently in the world of Victorian patriarchy.[3] As Nina Auerbach observes in her study, "the shifting idea of female communities survives beyond its problematical realization, and as art gives it body, it becomes part of the history it opposes and improves."[4] Trollope's group of ladies living happily together in Paris was her contribution to a new tradition depicting a self-sufficient woman's reality apart from men.

Chapter Seven
Conclusion
Domestic Relationships

When Dr. Jeune, the Head of Pembroke College, Oxford, and subsequently Bishop of Peterborough, first met Frances Trollope in Florence, he described the famous authoress, then in her seventies, to his wife with some surprise: "I dined with the Trollopes last night. I expected to find Mrs. Trollope epigrammatic,—I found her clever, intelligent, and domestic."[1] For her wit and satiric thrust of mind he had come prepared, but not for their combination with an assortment of traits he could sum up only in the century's word reserved for females, *domestic*. Indeed, Trollope's final achievement as a writer cannot be considered apart from her life as wife and mother of a large and often troubled family. Later, when either of her sons wrote of their mother's professional or private virtues, the two were inseparably combined. Her son Tom described her happy nature, "happier still in the conscious exercise of the power of making others happy."[2] Anthony spoke of "the mixture of joviality and industry which formed her character. . . . Even when she was at work," he recalled, "the laughter of those she loved was a pleasure to her."[3] Despite some recent feminist theory that extensive family responsibilities stifle artistic creativity, a blend of the intellectual and the domestic would remain Frances Trollope's trademark to the end of her life.

Trollope was also an intensely gregarious woman who loved the company of many friends. She had not only written about the importance of the female community, but had lived it herself. Her closest and most enduring friends had always been women. When a housewife at Harrow, she had enjoyed having young girls to visit her. She made countless trips to Exeter and London in those days, keeping close to her female circle of friends, aunts, childhood girl-friends, and neighbors, as well as to a more intellectual set of writers, actresses, and artists. She took up the cause of women friends in trouble: Madame Fauche, the consul's wife at Bruges, and Rosina

Bulwer, both of them enmeshed in difficult marital problems. Even the cataleptic Okey sisters, exploited by their friend Dr. Elliotson, came under her care. She was also fascinated by successful women, by Frances Wright, Mary Russell Mitford, and Laetitia Landon. She enjoyed friendships with the illustrious: Princess Melanie, Metternich's wife, Madame Recamier, and Madame de Chauteaubriand. Her lifelong association with the Garnett sisters was central to all their lives, sustaining Frances Trollope first, in her troubled days in America, and Julia and Harriet later, when they coped with the problems of their lives, one as a transplanted English wife in Germany, the other as aspiring but unsuccessful author in Paris. Their letters to each other were laced throughout with longings to be together, even while their fates had ordained otherwise. They had all shared similar pains and joys, and later Frances would draw on this common female experience for the creation of her many heroines.[4]

To be valued by friends is a great, though not uncommon achievement. Frances Trollope was also beloved by her children. For as long as each of them lived, she remained a devoted mother, sensitive to their wants, always "interruptable." Both her sons wrote autobiographies in which they paid high tribute to their mother. She was Tom's lifelong companion, friend to his first wife and literary inspiration to his second, who never met her. Anthony's relationship with his mother, so often misunderstood, was enormously fruitful. In his autobiography he emphasized her "power of self-sacrifice." She never strove to make her children feel guilty about all she did to keep the family together, nor did she ever express the need to "find herself" outside the responsibilities to them. Anthony wrote:

Now and again there would arise a feeling that it was hard upon my mother that she should have to do so much for us, that we should be idle while she was forced to work so constantly; but we should probably have thought more of that had she not taken to work as though it were the recognized condition of life for an old lady of 55.[5]

Only two of her children outlived her: she nursed all the others in their last illnesses, even Cecilia's which brought the seventy-year-old mother to England's Lake District from Florence, during the revolution-torn year of 1848.

Yet, through all her troubles, she never lost her sense of balance or fundamental joy in living. As Tom remarked, after the terrible death of Henry in 1834, "her mind was one of the most extraordinarily constituted in regard to recuperative power and the capacity of throwing off sorrow that I ever knew or read of." She seemed constitutionally able to celebrate life and not dwell on losses. "She owed herself to the living, and refused to allow unavailing regret for those who had been taken from her to incapacitate her for paying that debt to the utmost."[6] This temperament, oriented more toward thinking of others than herself, also helped her handle her literary success when it came so swiftly and unexpectedly. Her head remained unturned by the fame that followed the publication of her first book. Indeed, as one of her friends remembered, "She was alone amongst the female authoresses of the 'thirties and 'forties to give herself no airs." She was "in no sense a poseuse, but just a . . . good-natured kind of well-bred hen-wife, fond of a joke and not troubled with squeamishness."[7]

It could be said of her that she was thoroughly unconventional, both in the quality of her thought and in her personal habits, a dangerous combination for the early Victorian period. She certainly shocked the Americans, not only with her book, but even more with her behavior. In a good example of the *ad feminam* attacks she endured throughout her life, the *Cincinnati Chronicle and Literary Gazette* noted on the publication of her book: "Her whole appearance and conduct corresponded to her name. She was an impudent kind of man-woman, of vulgar exterior both in person and dress, of forward manners, and altogether just such a woman as no man could choose as the mentor of either daughters or sons."[8] Repeatedly, the word *vulgar* was used to describe her, yet there is no note in her personal life or professional writings that would today draw such an appellation. In the 1830s the word was synonymous with free, frank, and unconventional attitudes, particularly in women. To act or speak in any way at odds with the canons of female decorum was to be "vulgar"[9] Indeed, when Elizabeth and Robert Browning later met Frances Trollope in Florence, they were surprised to find her charming and cultured, not at all like the reputation she had been given by the reviewers. She was for the most part unconcerned about such detraction. In part, her stoicism stemmed from the age at which she began her literary labors.

Essentially, she had lived two lives—the first fifty years as daughter, wife, and mother, the last third, as writer and worker. And starting at age fifty-three, she left behind her thirty-four novels, six travel books, and a respectable achievement as a pioneering writer. She deserves a recognized place in the history of English literature. In large part, her ability to accomplish so much while still leading a rich and complicated domestic life, often filled with tragic troubles, is due to her energy, intensity, and work habits. Virginia Woolf has said that a woman, in order to write, needs a little money and a room of her own. Frances Trollope had neither when she started. What she did develop were working habits which enabled her to carve time and space from each day so as to accomplish what was needed. As she herself described her routine: "I get up at half-past four every morning, and get nearly the whole of my day's [writing] task accomplished before breakfast."[10] Whether she was in her own home or elsewhere, this schedule was rigorously maintained. As her daughter-in-law observed, "It was her habit of early rising, which alone made it possible for her to perform so much literary labour, without obtruding it on the rest of the world, or in any way interfering with the daily routine of other people's lives."[11] Again, her ability to combine her own needs with respect for "other people's lives" stands out as her special achievement. Tom remembered the gaiety of their home life, which was never dimmed either by domestic or professional troubles. "She seemed always ready to take part in all the fun and amusement that was going on; and was the first to plan dances, and charades, and picnics, and theatricals on a small and unpretending scale. But five o'clock of every morning saw her at her desk; and the production of the series of novels . . . never ceased."[12]

Her Pioneering Nature

While Trollope wrote no "great novels," she was a path-breaking author in a number of important ficitonal areas. In thus opening up more possibilities to fiction, she influenced the major novelists and deserves a significant place in the traditional nineteenth-century literary landscape.

Social Reform Fiction. First, she was an early explorer of controversial social problems across a whole range of subjects. She was surely in the forefront of the so-called "epic age" of women's literature, those nineteenth-century female authors who changed the world with their *Jane Eyres* and *Uncle Tom's Cabins*. Four of her books were significant "novels with a purpose."[13] She wrote the first antislavery novel (*Jonathan Jefferson Whitlaw*) and the first full-length exposure of evangelical excesses (*The Vicar of Wrexhill*). Her factory novel (*Michael Armstrong*) depicted child labor and the industrial and slum areas of England fifteen years before Dickens attacked the "dark satanic mills." *Jessie Phillips* offered the first fictional assault on the injustices of the New Poor Law, especially its discrimination against women.

These four novels, written over a ten-year period, straddled the decade in which fiction came of age as a serious art form. In rendering these "repulsive subjects" with such unrelieved vigor, Frances Trollope bore the front line of attack by reviewers, accustomed to the light popular fiction that had dominated the 1830s.

Travel Books.   Trollope's next claim to distinction is as an innovator in the travel-book genre. Her controversial *Domestic Manners of the Americans* helped revitalize an old form and established patterns for subsequent generations of commentators. While most early nineteenth-century travelers had emphasized facts, figures, and landscapes, Trollope concentrated on people and imbued her accounts with the techniques of fiction. Her travel books featured a strong narrator, a variation of the intrusive author, who provided interpretations and opinions. She also shaped a coherent plot line in which the author herself was sometimes heroine of the piece. Her people were sharply drawn individuals, some even stylized to represent social attitudes or ideas. Indeed, in her changing panoramas, people were the most important part.

Her unusual approach was sometimes misunderstood by critics who sought "not a fiction but truth," or "a specimen of mind, not imagination." Yet her accounts are now all the more valuable and stand out from those volumes of the hordes of forgotten nineteenth-century travelers precisely because of their decided personal views and the heightenings of the artist. And so, while one reviewer bristled at Frances Trollope and Dickens (*American Notes*, 1842), with whom she was often paired, as "these *outside* travelers" who gave only "their peculiar mode of seeing," these individual, experiential approaches to the reporting of travel have proven lasting, valuable, and influential to an age that has learned how the data of statistics and dry facts serve often to obscure rather than to clarify vision.[14]

To this day, her work on America remains the starting point for commentators on the United States. Though American critics and historians have called its author everything from "a wandering huzzy who chose to build bazaars" to a "censorious harridan, determined at all costs to vent an unreasonable prejudice against us," the accuracy of her observations is beyond dispute. Her books about her continental travels, while less well known and controversial, are also valuable documents of social history, useful both to the professional historian and any reader interested in re-creating a world now long lost.[15] The explanation for these successes, except for the last book on Italy, lies in her vivid involvement with the people she came to see and describe.

Characterizations of Women.   In addition to opening up the novel to social realism and rejuvenating the travel book genre, Trollope's creation of a new kind of female character was instrumental in breaking down nineteenth-century stereotypes about the heroine. When she began writing novels, the conventional heroine was a dependent woman who needed and sought male support. She was governed by emotions, not reason, and "would never be as clever as a clever man."[16] Of course, her natural destiny was marriage. Among these consistent early Victorian representations of the heroine as young, beautiful, religious, and submissive, Trollope's ladies, self-confident and aggressive, stride with authority through her pages, evolving steadily toward greater independence and initiative.

Trollope first gave women resourceful and manipulative roles in reform fiction, where female characters were the primary agents of change, in a period when real women had no political influence or even the vote. Next, she expanded the feminine picaresque, making her heroine a middle-class, middle-aged woman in search of her fortunes on the road. Then she made "marriageship" her subject, unveiling the hunt for a husband as pursued by so many of the century's "redundant" females in all its desperation and nastiness.[17] Her fortune-hunter characters viewed men frankly in terms of money and made no pretenses about feelings, while boldly and without self-delusions playing the parts men had created for them. If the world was a money-grubbing place and everyone had a price, then women had better make the best of their imprisonment in it, to survive and endure. In her late fiction she brought her mature women forward into the main plots with refreshing independence from men and a newly discovered sisterly feeling toward other women. Trol-

lope's writings constitute a broad opus devoted to exploring the
manifold possibilities for female lives.

Frances Trollope and the Critics

Critics and reviewers of her own time were alive to her innovations
and bristled with anger at her daring female characterizations. Her
daughter-in-law later marveled at the rough critical abuses she had
endured: "Those who demand for women's work a fair field and no
favour—could certainly not have complained that Mrs. Trollope
was treated with any contemptuous indulgence by reason of her sex.
The critics, big and little, who disliked her writings, belaboured
them as heartily as though she had a man—perhaps even a little
more heartily . . . to a flattering point of ruthlessness."[18] There
was a double standard in nineteenth-century book reviewing, and
Trollope encountered it all across her career. "A woman was sup-
posed to stay strictly within the limits of female delicacy in subject
and style: in return she could expect from her reviewer the gallant
treatment that a gentleman owes a lady."[19] Again and again Trollope
offended against the required delicacy for daring to treat subjects
reserved for male authors and for venturing to create new characters
and styles inappropriate to the current mode.

While critics did not yet agree about all the formal aspects of the
relatively new fictional art, they insisted on purity of tone, language,
and characterization. One twentieth-century commentator, working
through the criticism of the 1830s and 1840s repeatedly found the
words "unrefined" or "low" applied to realistic writing, from Fielding to Dickens.[20] Fiction should teach and be elevating. R. H.
Horne, in his 1844 book defining the "new spirit of the age,"
singled out Frances Trollope's works with a vengeance. He wrote:
"Her constitutional coarseness is the natural element of a low popularity, and is sure to pass for cleverness, shrewdness, and strength,
where cultivated judgment and chaste inspiration would be thrown
away." Of her style, he complained that her own personality was
too evident: "The predominant flavor is Trollope still." Her characters were "hideous and revolting" and seemed "to be eternally
bullying each other. . . . Her low people are sunk deeper than the
lowest depths, as if they had been bred in and in, to the last dregs.
Nothing can exceed the vulgarity of Mrs. Trollope's mob of characters." When her defenders pointed to the predominant realism

("We have heard it urged on behalf of Mrs. Trollope that her novels are, at all events, drawn from life."), the answer of Horne and others like him was simple: "So are sign paintings."[21]

Yet what angered the critics appealed to her public. She knew the craft and had become "a very skillfull bookmaker" with a large following. Aware of the connection between her fame and these often unpleasant notices, she learned a healthy objectivity. As she once remarked of a particularly vituperative review, "It will only help the sales go on." Disregarding the fierce critical attacks her works often provoked, she persevered in her vision. She had no doubt of its truth, for her own life and sturdy personality had been a source book for the long gallery of heroines, many of whom manifested their creator's robust and energetic womanhood in ways as yet unexplored, even by greater writers. Ironically, it is surprising that most of the recent commentators on women writers and the female literary imagination in the nineteenth century have ignored Trollope's contributions in developing new and complex characterizations of women.[22] Castigated in her time for vices which have come to be hailed as virtues, Trollope still awaits the critical recognition she deserves.

Such recognition must include both her considerable achievements as a literary innovator and the inspirational quality of her life. In her time, her life and works influenced her contemporaries and spurred her son Anthony on to a career as a great novelist.[23] In his autobiography Anthony Trollope enumerated with pride his mother's 114 volumes "of which the first was not written till she was fifty. Her career offers great encouragement to those who have not begun early in life, but are still ambitious to do something before they depart hence."[24] To all who read or write, the life and works of Frances Trollope can be energizing, as is demonstrable in this recent tribute from an American poet.

FLU

The windows glow and fade with fever.
I lie in bed reading. And each time a character destroys his life
It makes me sick. "Don't drink!" I groan at Dick Diver
"Can't you see I have a fever?" But he doesn't listen
And ends up poor and lonely, near Buffalo
Where the sky is always gray with driven snow.

So for health I read about Mrs. Trollope
A woman whose life-line keeps rising right to the end.
In my fever dreams I run up to her in her tattered black cloak
On the streets of Cincinnati. How's it going?
She laughs and says all this may look like suffering
But will soon be sold in the literary marketplace of the 19th century.
Her books come out. She writes them before dawn when her children
    are dying.
She's ill once, near Baltimore, but never again.

Until she forgets everything: England, the swamps of Tennessee,
Her crazy and unpleasant husband, her children with weak lungs
And well-satisfied she dies. Not lonely in Buffalo
But cherished and pleasantly out of her mind in sunny Florence.
She gets a good grade for life.

At night my fever passes like death
And I am reborn into a November of my own century
Books to write, and people to meet
As soon as I can throw off the bed clothes and begin.

                                              Alan Feldman[25]

Notes and References

Preface

1. Frances Eleanor Trollope, *Frances Trollope: Her Life and Literary Work from George III to Victoria*, 2 vols. (London, 1895); Thomas Adolphus Trollope, *What I Remember* (New York, 1888); Anthony Trollope, *An Autobiography*, 2 vols. (1883; reprint ed., London, 1961).

2. Michael Sadleir, *Trollope: a Commentary* (New York, 1947), p. 113.

Chapter One

1. Miriam Leranbaum, " 'Mistresses of Orthodoxy': Education in the Lives and Writings of Late Eighteenth-Century English Women Writers," *Proceedings of the American Philosophical Society* (August 1977), pp. 281–301. Clara Reeve (1729–1807) was a novelist and Anna Barbauld (1743–1825) a poet and devotional writer.

2. The forty-three courtship letters are currently housed in the Robert H. Taylor Collection, at Princeton University Library.

3. Trollope, *What I Remember,* pp. 41–42; and Trollope, *An Autobiography,* p. 28; hereafter cited as TAT, and AT.

4. Anna W. Merivale, *Family Memorials* (Exeter: Thomas Upward, 1884), p. 238. Entry for 11 February 1822.

5. *The Friendships of Mary Russell Mitford,* ed. A. G. K. L'Estrange, 2 vols. (New York, 1882), 1:160.

6. Frances Trollope's La Grange diary is currently located in the Anthony Trollope Collection at the University of Illinois Library, Urbana, Ill. The quotation is from AT, p. 28.

7. Wright to Harriet and Julia Garnett, 8 June 1825. This letter is part of an important and extensive correspondence preserved by Julia Garnett Pertz, which was made available to the author by her great-granddaughter, Dr. Cecilia Payne-Gaposchkin. The entire collection, the Garnett-Pertz collection (hereafter cited as GPC), is currently housed at the Houghton Library, Harvard University. The author wishes to express her gratitude to Dr. Gaposchkin's daughter, Mrs. Katherine Haramundanis, who is the present owner of the collection, for permission to quote from the letters.

8. Information from Frances Trollope's notebooks, currently housed in the Lilly Library of Indiana University. Some excerpts have been printed in Donald Smalley's edition of *Domestic Manners* (New York, 1949), pp. 28–29.

9. Advertisement for the Infernal Regions, from Cincinnati Historical Society.

10. Captain Frederick Marryat, *Diary in America* (London, 1839; reprint ed., London: Nicholas Vane, 1960) pp. 271–62, found Frances Trollope's representations of the city's manners and customs "probably more correct than the present inhabitants of the city will allow."

11. For a fuller description of the Bazaar, see Helen Heineman, *Mrs. Trollope: The Triumphant Feminine in the Nineteenth Century* (Athens, Ohio, 1979), pp. 59–67. For a discussion of the Bazaar's potential, see Helen Heineman, "Angel of Faneuil Hall," *Harvard Magazine* (March-April 1979), pp. 50–55.

12. Advertisement for an unnamed newspaper, 22 January 1830, file in the Cincinnati Historical Society.

13. See Barbara Welter, "The Cult of True Womanhood: 1820–1860," *American Quarterly* (1966), pp. 151–74.

14. Frances Eleanor Trollope, *Frances Trollope: Her Life and Literary Work* 2 vols. (London, 1895), 1:128–31, hereafter cited as FET.

15. TAT, p. 163; and AT, p. 21.

16. For a study of the relationships among this circle of women, see Helen Heineman, *Restless Angels* (Athens, Ohio, 1983).

17. Basil Hall to Frances Trollope, 21 January 1833, in FET, 1:173–75.

18. Trollope to John Murray, 15 October 1833, Archives of John Murray, London; hereafter cited as JMA.

19. FET, 1:169.

20. FET, 1:170. She also published a short poem, *The Mother's Manual* in 1833.

21. AT, p. 23.

22. Trollope to John Murray, 22 April 1834, JMA.

23. FET, 1:199.

24. AT, p. 27.

25. AT, pp. 24–25.

26. AT, p. 27.

27. The quotation is Trollope's own, as she describes the literary heroine Mrs. Sherborne in *Charles Chesterfield* (1841).

28. FET, 2:54–55.

29. Ibid., p. 100.

30. Ibid., p. 147.

31. Ibid., p. 166.

32. Ibid., p. 173.

33. Ibid., p. 177.

34. Ibid., p. 223.

35. Ibid., p. 242–44.

36. Ibid., p. 279.
37. Ibid., 261.

Chapter Two

1. FET, 1:161.
2. Because of the numerous editions of *Domestic Manners,* all references in the text henceforth will be by chapter number in parentheses.
3. For a fuller treatment of this subject, see Heineman, *Mrs. Trollope,* pp. 85–99.
4. See Helen Heineman, "Three Victorians in the New World: America in the works of Frances Trollope, Charles Dickens, and Anthony Trollope" (Ph.D. Dissertation, Cornell University, 1967). The quotation is from Frances Trollope to Julia Pertz, 27 June 1832, GPC.
5. Cf. *Domestic Manners* (Chap. 32) and *Refugee* (2:63 and 79).
6. *Refugee,* 1:29. Cf. *Domestic Manners* (Chap. 12); for the Burns hearthside, cf. *Refugee* (1:48–49) and *Domestic Manners* (Chap. 5); for Niagara, cf. *Refugee* (2:86 ff.) and *Domestic Manners* (Chap. 33).
7. *Refugee* 1:78 and 84. Cf. *Domestic Manners* (Chap. 9).
8. Smalley's introductory essay to *Domestic Manners,* pp. 21–22. For the Sam Patch story, cf. *Refugee* (2:59) and *Domestic Manners* (Chap. 32).
9. Cf. *Refugee* (2:3–5 and 113) and *Domestic Manners* (Chaps. 9 and 32).
10. Quotations from *The Refugee* and all other books by Mrs. Trollope will be cited in the text hereafter by volume and page number in parentheses.
11. Quoted in Smalley's introduction to *Domestic Manners,* p. xviii. Cf. *Refugee* 2:101.
12. For parallels, see *Refugee* 1:75–77, and *Domestic Manners,* Chap. 19.
13. Henry James, *Partial Portraits* (London: Macmillan & Co., 1888), pp. 120–21.
14. Trollope to Julia Pertz, 23 August 1833, GPC. *The Abbess* is discussed below, pp. 82–83.
15. See the unsigned review, "German Tourists," *Westminister Review* 22 (1835):511–20.
16. Cf. Sir Arthur Brooke Faulkner, *Visit to Germany and the Low Countries in the years 1829, 1830, and 1831* (London: Bentley, 1833). Frances Trollope had read Faulkner's account. See Frances Trollope to John Murray, 13 January 1834, JMA.
17. For a fuller treatment of this theme, see Heineman, *Mrs. Trollope,* pp. 124–27.
18. Unsigned review of *Belgium and Western Germany* in *Spectator* 7 (1834):684.

19. Trollope to John Murray, 22 July 1834, JMA.

20. Trollope to Richard Bentley, 24 June 1835, Robert H. Taylor Collection, Princeton University Library.

21. Unsigned review of *Paris and the Parisians* in *Spectator* 9 (1836):40.

22. Unsigned review of *Paris and the Parisians* in *The New Monthly Magazine* 46 (1836):239.

23. Because of the various editions, references to *Paris and the Parisians* will be to individual letters, which serve as chapters, cited by arabic numerals in parentheses in the text.

24. *New Monthly Magazine* 46 (1836):239.

25. See Cesar Grana's use of *Paris and the Parisians* in his *Bohemian Versus Bourgeois: French Society and the French Man of Letters in the 19th Century* (New York: Basic Books, 1964), pp. 17, 22, 43, 74–75.

26. Memorandum of an agreement between Frances Trollope and Richard Bentley, 27 April 1836, British Museum, ADD 46612, f. 240.

27. Trollope to Richard Bentley, 27 February 1837, TCP.

28. Unsigned review of *Vienna and the Austrians* in *Athenaeum* 538 (1838):113–14 and 139–40.

29. Unsigned review of *A Visit to Italy* in *Athenaeum* 781 (1842):884–85.

Chapter Three

1. Hugh Blair's *Rhetoric* (1783), an authoritative work in Frances Trollope's time, dismissed the novel in three pages as more often tending "to dissipation and idleness than to any good purpose." George Ford, *Dickens and His Readers: Aspects of Novel Criticism Since 1836* (New York: Norton, 1965), p. 24. Cf. "Silly Novels by Lady Novelists," *Westminster Review* 66 (1856), in *Essays of George Eliot,* ed. Thomas Pinney (London: Routledge & Kegan Paul, 1963), pp. 300–24.

2. Unsigned article, "The Lady Novelists of Great Britain," in *Gentlemen's Magazine* 194 (1853):18–19.

3. William Makepeace Thackeray, review of Lever's *St. Patrick's Eve,* in *Morning Chronicle,* 3 April 1845, reprinted in Gordon N. Ray, ed., *William Makepeace Thackeray's Contributions to the "Morning Chronicle"* (Urbana: University of Illinois Press, 1955), p. 71.

4. Quotation is from Inga-Stina Ewbank, *Their Proper Sphere: A Study of the Brontë Sisters as Early Victorian Novelists* (London: Scandinavian University Books, 1966), p. 14. Ewbank, while praising Charlotte Tonna, Harriet Martineau, and Elizabeth Gaskell, criticizes Frances Trollope as having "a finger on the pulse of the public and an eye on the seller's market, rather than gifts or inclinations in any one particular literary direction." Such criticism is unfair for two reasons. It overlooks Frances Trollope's numerous innovations and daring themes, which won her more

criticism than approbation. Secondly, this criticism implies that feeling for the pulse of the public is somehow a disgrace, yet all great writers—including Trollope's contemporary Charles Dickens—have searched for this same pulse.

5. For a fuller discussion of the role settings played in this novel, see Heineman, *Mrs. Trollope*, pp. 145–46.

6. Unsigned reviews of *Whitlaw* in *Spectator* 9 (1836):634–35; and *Athenaeum*, no. 453 (1836), pp. 462–63. For a typical slave narrative, see Linda Brent, *Incidents in the Life of a Slave Girl* (New York: Harcourt Brace, 1973).

7. Unsigned review of *The Vicar*, in *Athenaeum*, no. 517 (1837), p. 708. Cf. unsigned review in *Westminster Review* 38 (1838):115: "[*The Vicar*] is written with as hearty and thorough-going a *gusto* for what is repulsive and horrible, as if its authoress had drunk of the witch broth."

8. After 1856, clerical novels, with a focus on female religious folly and filled with vicars who "lead ladies up the garden" and seduce parish girls, were commonplace. See Margaret Maison, *Search Your Soul Eustace: A Survey of the Religious Novel in the Victorian Age* (London: Sheed & Ward, 1961).

9. Unsigned review of *The Vicar*, in *Dublin Review* 7 (1839):247.

10. "Clerical beastliness" is Maison's term, *Eustace*, pp. 83–84. Quotation is from unsigned review of *The Vicar* in *Athenaeum*, no. 517 (1837), p. 708.

11. Unsigned review of *The Vicar* in *Examiner*, no. 1548 (1837), 628.

12. *The Northern Star*, 2 March 1839.

13. For a complete discussion of Trollope's use of the Blincoe pamphlet, see Heineman, *Mrs. Trollope*, 177–79. The Blincoe pamphlet has recently been republished by Kenneth E. Carpenter, ed., *The Ten Hours Movement in 1831 and 1832* (New York: Arno Press, 1972).

14. *Michael Armstrong* appeared first in monthly parts from 26 February 1839. In 1840 both a one-volume and three-volume edition appeared. Because of the broad availability of the one-volume edition, I have cited from that version.

15. Unsigned review of *Michael Armstrong* in *New Monthly Magazine* 57 (1839):286.

16. Charlotte Elizabeth Tonna was the author of *Helen Fleetwood*, an industrial novel which was serialized in *Christian Lady's Magazine* in 1839–1840, a few months after the appearance of *Michael Armstrong*. Tonna's solution for the conditions of the poor was Christian resignation. For discussions of the industrial novel, see David Skilton, *The English Novel: Defoe to the Victorians* (New York, 1977), and Ivanka Kovačević, ed., *Fact*

Into Fiction: English Literature and the Industrial Scene, 1750–1850 (Leicester, 1975).

17. For confirmation of Trollope's descriptions, see William Rathbone Greg's pamphlet, "An enquiry into the state of the manufacturing population and the causes and cures of the evils therein existing" (1831), reprinted in *The Ten Hours Movement* (1972); Fredrick Engels, *The Condition of the Working Class in England,* reprinted by W. O. Henderson and W. H. Chaloner, eds. (New York: Macmillan, 1958); J. T. Ward, *The Factory Movement,* 1830–1855 (London: Macmillan, 1962). Only the rather superficial article by W. H. Chaloner ("Mrs. Trollope and the Early Factory System," *Victorian Studies* 4 (1960):159–66, suggests that Frances Trollope exaggerated.

18. See J. C. Gill, *The Ten-Hours Parson: Christian Social Action in the Eighteen-thirties* (London: S.P.C.K., 1959). For the Trollopes's visit with Parson Bull, see TAT, pp. 281–82.

19. Her description of this degradation is worth quoting: "Then comes a state of deeper degradation still. The father is idle, for often he can get no work, and it is to the labour of his little ones that he looks for bread. Nature recoils from the spectacle of their unnatural o'erlaboured aspect as they return from their 13, 14, 15 hours of toil. He has not nerve to look upon it, and creeps to the gin-shops till they are hid in bed. The mother sees it all and sternly screws her courage to the task of lifting their bruised and weary limbs upon their bed of straw, putting into their mouths the food she has prepared . . . and preparing herself to wake before the sun . . . and drive them forth again to get her food" (pp. 203–4).

20. For a discussion of this plate, see Chaloner, "Mrs. Trollope," p. 166.

21. Roger P. Wallins, "Mrs. Trollope's Artistic Dilemma in *Michael Armstrong,*" *Ariel* 8 (1977): pp. 8 ff.

22. Unsigned review of *Michael Armstrong* in *Athenaeum,* no. 615 (1839), p. 587.

23. For a fuller discussion of the bastardy clauses and Trollope's use of this theme, see Helen Heineman, "Frances Trollope's *Jessie Phillips:* Sexual Politics and The New Poor Law," *International Journal of Women's Studies* 1 (1978); and Ursula Henriques, "Bastardy and the New Poor Law," *Past and Present,* no. 37 (1967); and Sally Mitchell, "Lost Women: Feminist Implications of the Fallen in Works by Forgotten Women Writers of the 1840's," *University of Michigan Papers in Women's Studies* 1 (1974).

24. *Jessie Phillips* appeared in monthly parts beginning 31 December 1842. It appeared in both a one-volume and a three-volume edition in 1843. Because of the broad availability of the one-volume version, I have cited from that edition.

25. For the debate over the New Poor Law, see Cecil Driver, *Tory Radical: the Life of Richard Oastler* (New York: Oxford University Press, 1946); Mark Blaug, "The Poor Law Report Reexamined," *Journal of Economic History* 24 (1964); Ursula Henriques, "How Cruel was the Victorian Poor Law?", *Historical Journal* 11 (1968); and Thomas Mackay, *A History of the English Poor Law*, 3 vols. (New York: Putnam's Sons, 1900).

26. Unsigned review of *Jessie Phillips* (together with *Martin Chuzzlewit*) in *Spectator* 16 (1843):17–18.

Chapter Four

1. See the excellent study by Sandra Gilbert and Susan Gubar, *The Madwoman in the Attic: The Woman Writer and the Nineteenth-Century Literary Imagination* (New Haven: Yale University Press, 1979).

2. J. M. S. Tompkins, *The Popular Novel In England, 1770–1800* (Lincoln: University of Nebraska Press, 1961), p. 243.

3. Unsigned review of *The Abbess* in *Spectator* 6 (1833):526–27.

4. Unsigned review of *Tremordyn Cliff* in *Athenaeum*, no. 411 (1835), pp. 692–93; and *Spectator* 8 (1835):855.

5. Unsigned reviews of *The Ward* in *John Bull* 22 (1842):153; and *Athenaeum*, no. 754 (1842), p. 312.

6. Margaret Dalziel, *Popular Fiction 100 Years Ago: An Unexplored Track of Literary History* (London: Cohen & West, 1957), p. 113.

7. See Elizabeth Sanford, *Woman in Her Social and Domestic Character*, 5th ed. (Boston: Otis, Broaders & Co., 1843); Sarah Ellis, *The Women of England: Their Social Duties and Domestic Habits* (New York: Appleton & Co., 1843).

8. The first Thackeray quotation is from his review of *Jerome Paturot* in *Fraser's Magazine* 28 (1843): 350; the second is from his letter to Lucy Baxter, 11 March 1853, quoted in Miriam Allot, *Charlotte Brontë: Jane Eyre and Villette, a Casebook* (London: Macmillan, 1973), p. 93. For good discussions of the conventional heroine, see Robert Palfrey Utter and Gwendolyn Bridges Needham, *Pamela's Daughters* (New York: Macmillan, 1936), pp. 372 ff., and Patricia Thomson, *The Victorian Heroine* (London: Oxford University Press, 1956), pp. 167 ff.

9. Gilbert and Gubar, *Madwoman in the Attic*, p. 76.

10. *Barnabys in America*, 1:2.

11. *Widow Barnaby*, 2:87. Cf. *The Widow Married*, 3:121–22 for similar sentiments.

12. Unsigned review, London *Times*, 24 January 1839, and unsigned article, "Female Novelists: Part V: Mrs. Trollope," *New Monthly Magazine* 96 (1852):25.

13. *The Widow Married*, 1:193.

14. Unsigned article, "Modern Novelists—Great and Small," *Blackwood's Edinburgh Magazine* 77 (1855):355–56. For an analysis of the change in fictional treatment of women, which does not, however, discuss Frances Trollope's contribution, see Utter and Needham, *Pamela's Daughters,* passim.

15. *Blackwood's Edinburgh Magazine* 77 (1855):356.

Chapter Five

1. Both novels appeared in 12 monthly parts and both began to appear in July 1840. While several authors wrote serializations which overlapped to some extent, there can have been few with sufficient physical and creative energy to write two serializations simultaneously.

2. AT, p. 102.

3. Trollope's Mrs. Sherbourne no doubt provided her son Anthony with a model for Lady Carbury (*The Way We Live Now,* 1875). But while Anthony's heroine eventually marries and is freed from the exertions of a writing career, Frances Trollope's authoress successfully continues to dupe editor and public alike. See Heineman, *Mrs. Trollope,* p. 202.

4. Margaretta Hartley and her numerous successors obviously influenced Anthony Trollope's own creation of a series of vibrant, robust, and complex female characters (Lady Carbury, Madame Max Goessler, and the great Lady Glencora), especially his fine and sympathetically drawn fortune hunter, Arabella Trefoil (*The American Senator,* 1877). For a discussion of Trollope's influence on her son, see Heineman, *Mrs. Trollope,* pp. 202 ff.

5. Unsigned review of *The Blue Belles* in *Spectator* 15 (1842):42.

6. Unsigned review of *Young Love* in *John Bull,* 23 November 1844, p. 743.

7. Unsigned review of *The Laurringtons* in *Athenaeum,* no. 842 (1843), p. 1107.

8. See Gilbert and Gubar, *Madwoman in the Attic,* passim.

9. Unsigned reviews of *The Laurringtons* in *Dublin Review* 15 (1843):543; in *Athenaeum,* no. 842 (1843), p. 1107.

10. Unsigned review of *The Attractive Man* in *Literary Gazette,* no. 1501 (1845), pp. 700–1.

11. Unsigned review of *Three Cousins* in *John Bull,* 29 May 1847, p. 344, italics mine.

12. FET, 2:79–80.

13. I have been able to obtain only a one-volume edition of this novel, and cite from this version (London: J. & C. Brown & Co., n.d.); page references given in text.

14. See the discussion in Tompkins, *The Popular Novel,* pp. 54, 136.

15. See Gilbert and Gubar, *Madwoman in the Attic,* pp. 80–83.

16. Unsigned review of *Lottery of Marriage* in *John Bull,* 5 May 1849, p. 279.

17. For a discussion of this unusual genre, see "The Wicked Jesuit and Company" in Margaret Maison, *Search Your Soul, Eustace,* pp. 169–82; "The Catholics and Their Friends and Enemies" in Robert Lee Wolff, *Gains and Losses: Novels of Faith and Doubt in Victorian England* (New York: Garland, 1977), pp. 27–107, esp 38–40.

18. Unsigned review of *Father Eustace* in *New Monthly Magazine* 79 (1847):135.

19. Unsigned reviews of *The Robertses* in *Gentleman's Magazine* 26 (1846):179; in *John Bull* 26 (1846):247.

Chapter Six

1. Unsigned reviews of *Uncle Walter* in *John Bull* 33 (1852):396; in *Literary Gazette,* no. 1873 (1852), p. 906.

2. Unsigned reviews of *Uncle Walter* in *Athenaeum,* no. 1305 (1852), pp. 1169–1170; in *John Bull* 33 (1852):396.

3. For a general discussion of the role of sisterhood in Frances Trollope's own life, see Heineman, *Restless Angels.*

4. Nina Auerbach, *Communities of Women: An Idea in Fiction* (Cambridge: Harvard University Press, 1978), p. 30.

Chapter Seven

1. FET, 2:100.

2. TAT, pp. 489–90.

3. AT, p. 21.

4. See Heineman, *Restless Angels.*

5. AT, p. 21.

6. TAT, pp. 174–75, 207.

7. From the memoirs of Mrs. Lynn Lynton, cited in James Pope-Hennessy, *Anthony Trollope* (Boston: Little Brown, 1971), p. 34.

8. *Cincinnati Chronicle and Literary Gazette,* 23 June 1832.

9. Even the works of Charlotte Brontë were in her time consistently referred to by critics as "coarse" and "vulgar." For her struggle with the reviewers, see Ewbank, *Proper Sphere,* pp. 44–48.

10. FET, 1:320. In describing the female literary tradition in the English novel, Elaine Showalter (*A Literature of Their Own,* Princeton: Princeton University Press, 1977, p. 65 ff.) discusses the serious conflicts inherent for women writers in combining marriage and motherhood with a career in writing. She does not, however, analyze the specific means by which women like Elizabeth Gaskell and Frances Trollope managed to balance the claims of the domestic and the artistic roles.

11. FET, 2:43.

12. TAT, p. 208.

13. For a discussion of the "epic age," see chapter two in Ellen Moers, *Literary Women: The Great Writers* (New York: Doubleday, 1977). Moers gives only passing mention to Trollope's contributions.

14. Unsigned review of Charles Dickens's *American Notes* and Frances Trollope's *A Visit to Italy,* in "Superficial Traveling," *Dublin Review* 14 (1843):255–68).

15. See, for example, Cesar Grana's perceptive comment that Trollope's sharp observations bring "the life of the city closer to the grasp of the social historian" in *Bohemian Versus Bourgeois: French Society and the French Man of Letters in the 19th Century* (New York: Basic Books, 1964), p. 22. Cf. use of Frances Trollope in Henry T. Tuckerman, *America and Her Commentators* (New York, 1864); Allan Nevins, *America Through British Eyes* (Gloucester, Mass.: Peter Smith, 1968).

16. Margaret Dalziel, *Popular Fiction 100 Years Ago,* p. 90.

17. "There is an enormous and increasing number of single women in the nation . . . indicative of an unwholesome social state. . . . There are hundreds of thousands of women . . . who have to earn their own living, instead of spending and husbanding the earnings of men. . . . who, in place of completing, sweetening, and embellishing the existence of others, are compelled to lead an independent and incomplete existence of their own." William Rathbone Greg, "Why are Women Redundant?" in *Literary and Social Judgments* (Boston: James R. Osgood, 1873), pp. 274–308.

18. FET, 1:3; also 1:175, 214, 249.

19. Ewbank, *Proper Sphere,* p. 2. For a complete discussion of Victorian *ad feminam* criticism, see Showalter, *Literature of Their Own,* pp. 73 ff. She suggests Victorians were "responding to what seemed like a revolutionary, and in many ways a very threatening, phenomenon."

20. See George H. Ford, *Dickens and His Readers: Aspects of Novel Criticism since 1836* (Princeton: Princeton University Press, 1955), p. 33.

21. R. H. Horne, *New Spirit of the Age* (New York: J. C. Riker, 1844), pp. 239 ff.

22. Ewbank (*Proper Sphere,* pp. 13–14, 25–26), giving Trollope a page of space, deplores her tendency to keep "a finger on the pulse of the public and an eye on the seller's market," claiming the writer lacked "gifts or inclinations in any one particular literary direction," as if broad literary experimentation were a sin. This study denigrates female contributions to the social reform genre, contending that "not many women had enough experience of the other nation . . . to deal convincingly with the facts of a new society." Patricia Meyer Spacks (*The Female Imagination,* New York: Knopf, 1972), makes no mention of Trollope in her study of the creative expressions of women. Showalter *(Literature of Their Own)* includes only

two references to the Trollopes, but to Anthony's article excusing women from signing their published articles: "The nature of a woman is such that we admire her timidity and do not even regret her weakness." Showalter fails to comment on this extraordinary remark from the son of Frances Trollope. Moers *(Literary Women)* briefly refers to Trollope as an energetic writer passionately interested in reform, but concentrates instead on Mrs. Tonna. Gilbert and Gubar *(Madwoman in the Attic)* have a brilliant study, but do not include Trollope in their study of the female literary tradition.

23. As one of Anthony's friends and first biographers noted on this subject, "It will not be difficult when the proper place for doing so is reached, to find in Frances Trollope's volumes the germs from which grew some of Anthony Trollope's novels." Thomas Hay Sweet Escott, *Anthony Trollope: His Public Services, Private Friends and Literary Originals* (London: John Lane, 1913), p. 29. In fact, few commentators on Anthony have noted these connections with his mother.

24. AT, p. 28.

25. Unpublished poem by Alan Feldman, 1979. His collection of poems, *The Happy Genius* (New York: Sun Press, 1978), won the Elliston Award for 1978. In a slightly different version, "Flu" will be included in his forthcoming new collection.

Selected Bibliography

PRIMARY SOURCES

(Listed chronologically)

The Domestic Manners of the Americans. Illustrated by A. Hervieu. 2 vols. London: Whittaker, Treacher, 1832. Reprint, Donald Arthur Smalley, ed. New York: Alfred Knopf, 1949.

The Refugee in America: a Novel. 3 vols. London: Whittaker, Treacher, 1832.

The Mother's Manual: or Illustrations of Matrimonial Economy. An Essay in Verse. Illustrated by A. Hervieu. 1 vol. London: Treutel & Würtz & Richter, 1833.

The Abbess: A Romance. 3 vols. London: Whittaker, Treacher, 1833.

Tremordyn Cliff. 3 vols. London: Bentley, 1835.

Belgium and Western Germany in 1833: including Visits to Baden-Baden, Wiesbaden, Cassel, Hanover, the Harz Mountains, etc. etc. 2 vols. London: Bentley, 1836.

Paris and the Parisians in 1835. Illustrated by A. Hervieu. 2 vols. London: Bentley, 1836.

The Life and Adventures of Jonathan Jefferson Whitlaw: or Scenes on the Mississippi. Illustrated by A. Hervieu. 3 vols. London: Bentley, 1836. Reissued in 1857 under the title *Lynch Law.*

The Vicar of Wrexhill. Illustrated by A. Hervieu. 3 vols. London: Bentley, 1837.

Vienna and the Austrians. Illustrated by A. Hervieu. 2 vols. London: Bentley, 1838.

A Romance of Vienna. 3 vols. London: Bentley, 1838.

The Widow Barnaby. 3 vols. London: Bentley, 1839.

The Widow Married: A Sequel to The Widow Barnaby. Illustrated by R. W. Buss. 3 vols. London: Colburn, 1840.

The Life and Adventures of Michael Armstrong, the Factory Boy. Illustrated by A. Hervieu, R. W. Buss, and T. Onwhyn. Published in twelve monthly numbers from 1 March 1839 to 1 February 1840 by Colburn. First book edition in 3 vols. London: Colburn, [December] 1839, and in a one-volume edition [March] 1840.

One Fault: a Novel. 3 vols. London: Bentley, 1840.

Charles Chesterfield: or the Adventures of a Youth of Genius. Illustrated by "Phiz." 3 vols. London: Colburn, 1841.

The Ward of Thorpe Combe. 3 vols. London: Bentley, 1841. Reissued also in 1841 under the title *The Ward.*

The Blue Belles of England. 3 vols. London: Saunders and Otley, 1842.

A Visit to Italy. 2 vols. London: Bentley, 1842.

The Barnabys in America: or Adventures of the Widow Wedded. Illustrated by John Leech. 3 vols. London: Colburn, 1843.

Hargrave: or the Adventures of a Man of Fashion. 3 vols. London: Colburn, 1843.

Jessie Phillips: a Tale of the Present Day. Illustrated by John Leech. Published in eleven monthly parts from 31 December 1842 to 30 November 1843 by Colburn as *Jessie Phillips: a Tale of the New Poor Law.* First book edition in 3 vols. London: Colburn, 1843, and in a one-volume edition, 1844

The Laurringtons: or Superior People. 3 vols. London: Longman, Brown, Green and Longmans, 1844.

Young Love: a Novel. 3 vols. London: Colburn, 1844.

The Attractive Man. 3 vols. London: Colburn, 1844.

The Robertses on their Travels. 3 vols. London: Colburn, 1846.

Travels and Travelers: a Series of Sketches. 2 vols. London: Colburn, 1846.

Father Eustace: a Tale of the Jesuits. 3 vols. London: Colburn, 1847.

The Three Cousins. 3 vols. London: Colburn, 1847.

Town and Country: a Novel. 3 vols. London: Colburn, 1848. Reissued in 1857 under the title *Days of the Regency.*

The Young Countess: or Love and Jealousy. 3 vols. London: Colburn, 1848.

The Lottery of Marriage: a Novel. 3 vols. London: Colburn, 1849.

The Old World and the New: a Novel. 3 vols. London: Colburn, 1849.

Petticoat Government: a Novel. 3 vols. London: Colburn, 1850.

Mrs. Mathews, or Family Mysteries. 3 vols. London: Colburn, 1851.

Second Love, or Beauty and Intellect: a Novel. 3 vols. London: Colburn, 1851.

Uncle Walter: a Novel. 3 vols. London: Colburn, 1852.

The Young Heiress: a Novel. 3 vols. London: Hurst & Blackett, 1853.

The Life and Adventures of a Clever Woman. Illustrated with Occasional Extracts from her Diary. 3 vols. London: Hurst & Blackett, 1854.

Gertrude: or Family Pride. 3 vols. London: Hurst & Blackett, 1855.

Fashionable Life: or Paris and London. 3 vols. London: Hurst & Blackett, 1856.

SECONDARY SOURCES

1. Books and Parts of Books

Bigland, Eileen. *The Indomitable Mrs. Trollope.* New York: J. B.
    Lippincott Co., 1954. First modern biography of Trollope, full of
    invented fictional re-creations of her life passed off as factual. No
    critical attention to her works. A largely worthless account.

Heineman, Helen. *Mrs. Trollope: The Triumphant Feminine in the 19th
    Century.* Athens: Ohio University Press, 1979. Complete
    biographical study, based on extensive new and unpublished
    materials and a critical evaluation of all the author's works. Aided
    by financial documents and family correspondence, this biography
    corrects old errors about the Trollopes at Harrow and in Cincinnati
    and the relationship of Mrs. Trollope with her husband and
    family. As literary criticism, the book argues for recognition of
    Frances Trollope as a writer of seriousness and depth, with
    influence on the major directions of the nineteenth-century novel
    through her pioneering efforts in social reform and in developing
    new, complex characterizations of women.

————. *Restless Angels: The Friendship of Six Victorian Women.* Athens:
    Ohio University Press, 1983. The composite biography of a circle
    of early nineteenth-century women, one of whom was Frances
    Trollope. The book argues that the sisterhood these women created
    through a shared correspondence of twenty-five years was a crucial
    element in their attempts to find satisfying occupation, usefulness,
    and emotional satisfaction in combination with women's traditional
    roles.

Johnston, Johanna. *The Life, Manners, and Travels of Fanny Trollope: A
    Biography.* New York: Hawthorn Books, 1978. A fanciful and
    inaccurate repetition of older versions of Trollope's life, full of
    errors and misrepresentations.

Kovačević, Ivanka, ed., *Fact into Fiction: English Literature and the
    Industrial Scene, 1750-1850.* Leicester, England: Leicester
    University Press, 1975. Survey of the industrial theme in English
    fiction and anthology of various types of writing which reflect the
    impact of the Industrial Revolution. Treatment of *Michael
    Armstrong* and *Jessie Phillips* is superficial.

Pope-Hennessy, James. *Anthony Trollope.* Boston: Little Brown & Co.,
    1971. Repeats all the old stories about the Trollope family,
    including the mistakes about the American trip and the Bazaar.

Adds nothing to the reader's understanding or appreciation of
Frances Trollope's life or works.

Sadleir, Michael. *Trollope: a Commentary*. New York: Farrar, Straus &
Co., 1947. This elegant 1927 study (revised in 1947) restored
Anthony Trollope's stature as a novelist. The book's first quarter is
devoted to "Anthony's mother." Despite admiration for her
indomitable personal qualities, Sadleir is condescending toward her
intellectual accomplishments and literary efforts. His fine re-
creation of the Trollopes' family life and the American venture is
so persuasively presented that it has been adopted by all
subsequent commentators, despite its error on many important
points. Equally influential has been his dismissal of Frances
Trollope's literary importance: "Her writing began in desperate
necessity, continued as a good means to livelihood, and ended as
an agreeable habit . . . in consequence, she never became a
novelist of more than ephemeral significance. . . ."

Skilton, David. *The English Novel: Defoe to the Victorians*. New York:
Barnes & Noble, 1977. A good survey of the industrial novel in
England, including a discussion of *Michael Armstrong*.

Smalley, Donald, ed. *The Domestic Manners of the Americans by Frances
Trollope*. New York: Alfred Knopf, 1949. Introductory essay to
this edition of *Domestic Manners* includes information from
contemporary Cincinnati newspapers and the private notebooks of
the author. Without the evidence of Trollope's unpublished
personal letters, however, Smalley errs about many aspects of her
experiences, especially the motivation behind her American trip.

Trollope, Anthony. *An Autobiography*. 2 vols. Edinburgh, 1883.
Reprint (2 vols. in one). London: Oxford University Press, 1961.
Includes a chapter on his mother. While he gives high praise to
her happy personality, understated self-sacrifice, heroic
breadwinning, and successful mothering, he is condescending
about her novelistic ability. His account must be carefully balanced
with other evidence to determine the extent of Frances Trollope's
personal and professional influence on her son.

Trollope, Frances Eleanor. *Frances Trollope: Her Life and Literary Work
from George III to Victoria*. 2 vols. London: Bentley & Son, 1895.
Authorized biography by the second wife of Thomas Adolphus
Trollope. Although Frances Eleanor never knew her mother-in-law
personally, she used her husband's lifelong collection of family
letters as the basis of a lauditory "life and times" account. Because
many of the original sources from which she quotes extensively
have subsequently disappeared, this biography remains invaluable,
despite its lack of critical evaluation of Mrs. Trollope's works.

Trollope, Thomas Adolphus. *What I Remember.* New York: Harper & Bros., 1888. This autobiography by Trollope's eldest son and lifelong companion contains much first-hand information on her life, friends, and travels. An important source for Frances Trollope's early family life (often a corrective to Anthony's depictions) and for the later years in Florence. Like Anthony, Thomas Adolphus provides no discussion of his mother's literary works.

Tuckerman, Henry T. *America and Her Commentators, with a Critical Sketch of Travel in the United States.* New York: Charles Scribner, 1864. Cites Trollope's superior handling of narrative, lively, confident style, and remarkable powers of observation in accounting for the extraordinary contemporary popularity of *Domestic Manners.* While admitting the validity of the faults she recorded, he claims she did not "recognize the compensatory facts of American life" and failed to see any progress in the advance of democratic principles. Still, "few of the class of books to which it belongs are better worth reading now than this once famous record of Mrs. Trollope."

2. Articles

Abbott, Carl. "The Location and External Appearance of Mrs. Trollope's Bazaar." *Journal of the Society of Architectural Historians* 29 (1970):256–60. Claims that Trollope's Bazaar failed because she located it in a "retired" part of town, a quarter of a mile away from the commercial heart of Cincinnati. Criticizes the stylistic eclecticism of the building, calling it "an architectural monster" which stood out in "a city of brick boxes with Neoclassical trim."

Chaloner, W. H. "Mrs. Trollope and the Early Factory System." *Victorian Studies* 4 (1960):159–66. Admits Trollope's genuine humanitarian bent, but treats *Michael Armstrong* and her interest in factory reform as primarily a superficial search for a best seller. Cites harsh contemporary criticism of the novel and ignores its praise by recent historians because of Chaloner's bias against using novels as sources for social and economic history.

Flint, Timothy. "Travellers in America, etc." *Knickerbocker, or New York Monthly Magazine* 2 (1833):283–302. A presentation of Trollope's American travels and book by a contemporary who knew her during her Cincinnati residence. Biased and heavily saturated with sarcasm, the account concedes the relevance of many of Trollope's criticisms of American life. Originates the theory that *Domestic Manners* would have been a different book had its author been well received in America.

Griffin, Russell A. "Mrs. Trollope and the Queen City." *Mississippi Valley Historical Review* 37 (1950):289–302. Good but condescending account which in the absence of documents correctly questions previous assumptions about the precise goals of the American venture and which recognizes the improvisatory nature of the Bazaar.

Heineman, Helen. "The Angel of Faneuil Hall." *Harvard Magazine* 81 (March-April 1979):50–55. Analysis of Trollope's Bazaar as a center intended to revitalize Cincinnati's downtown district by bringing people together for shopping, entertainment, social intercourse, and culture. The Bazaar is described and fully analyzed as a prototype of planned urban environments in America, and the real reasons for its failure are presented. Argues that Boston's Quincy Market complex vindicates the validity of her ideas.

———. "Frances Trollope in the New World: *Domestic Manners of the Americans.*" *American Quarterly* 21 (1969):544–59. A close textual and stylistic analysis of Trollope's American travel book. Explains the popular appeal of the work, as well as the more enduring excellences which have made it so justifiably famous.

———. "Frances Trollope's *Jessie Phillips:* Sexual Politics and the New Poor Law." *International Journal of Women's Studies* 1 (January 1978):60–80. Shows Trollope interested in issues concerning the special problems of women in nineteenth-century society. Demonstrates that *Jessie Phillips* was an attack upon the sex bias of the New Poor Law of 1834, especially its bastardy clauses.

———. "Starving in that Land of Plenty: New Backgrounds to *Domestic Manners of the Americans.*" *American Quarterly* 24 (1972):643–60. The first discussion of Trollope's American experience based on her personal letters from America which reveal the motives (previously misunderstood) behind her decision to come to America, the length of her stay, and the writing of her book.

Lancaster, Clay. "The Egyptian Hall and Mrs. Trollope's Bazaar." *Magazine of Art* 43 (1950):94–99. Convincing examination of the architectural antecedents of the Bazaar, which defends its eclectic mixture of styles and contains a full description of the building (with conjectural drawings by the author) based on contemporary documents which are largely here reprinted. This otherwise careful account fails to appreciate the building's total conception and characterizes it as "a monument to the failure of ambitious enterprise."

Mitchell, Sally. "Lost Women: Feminist Implications of the Fallen in Works by Forgotten Women Writers of the 1840's." *University of*

Michigan Papers in Women's Studies 1 (June 1974):110–24.
Discusses Trollope's handling of emerging feminist issues and
concludes the law was not likely to be changed by depiction and
praise of strong women, but rather by emphasizing female
weakness, thereby "arousing the chivalry of male legislators."

Nisbet, Ada B. "Mrs. Trollope's *Domestic Manners*." *Nineteenth Century
Fiction* 4 (1949–1950):319–24. Review of Donald Smalley's
edition of *Domestic Manners*. Credits Trollope's book with setting
the pattern for all subsequent tourist commentaries on the United
States. Based on Smalley's sources, the article argues that *Domestic
Manners* was used by its publishers as Tory propaganda against the
English reform bills.

Tucker, Louis Leonard. "Cincinnati: Athens of the West, 1830–
1831." *Ohio History* 75 (1966):10–25. Details the devastating
effects of *Domestic Manners* upon the reputation of Cincinnati as
cultural center of the Ohio Valley. Attempts to establish the
validity of the city's claim to the title of "Athens of the West."
This defense is based almost exclusively on materials from later
periods of the city's life and is therefore irrelevant to Trollope's
claims that the cultural and intellectual life of Cincinnati in the
1827–1833 period was depressingly deficient.

Wallins, Roger P. "Mrs. Trollope's Artistic Dilemma in *Michael
Armstrong*." *Ariel: A Review of International English Literature* 8
(April 1977):5–15. A good evaluation of Trollope's success in
Michael Armstrong in writing good propaganda on the factory
conditions without sacrificing the artistic integrity of her work.
Four problems are isolated: integrating the two plot strands,
authorial intrusion, lengthy didactic dialogue, and stereotyped
characters. Examples of Trollope's successes (and failures) show that
she resolved the dilemma of the social novelist: propaganda vs. art.

Index

DATE DUE

DEMCO 38-297